GIGGLE WATER

INCLUDING ELEVEN FAMOUS
COCKTAILS OF THE MOST
EXCLUSIVE CLUB OF
NEW YORK

As Served Before the War

WHEN MIXING DRINKS WAS
AN ART

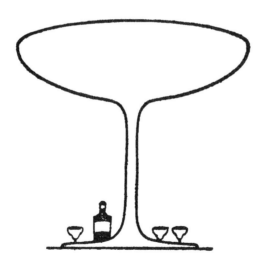

Martino Publishing
Mansfield Centre, CT
2015

Martino Publishing
P.O. Box 373,
Mansfield Centre, CT 06250 USA

ISBN 978-1-61427-906-8

© *2015 Martino Publishing*

Cover Design Tiziana Matarazzo

Printed in the United States of America On 100% Acid-Free Paper

GIGGLE WATER

INCLUDING ELEVEN FAMOUS
COCKTAILS OF THE MOST
EXCLUSIVE CLUB OF
NEW YORK

As Served Before the War

WHEN MIXING DRINKS WAS
AN ART

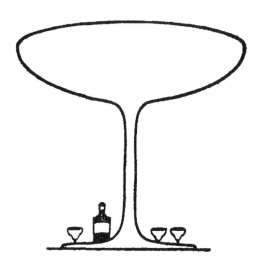

CHARLES S. WARNOCK

509 Fifth Avenue   New York

PRINTED IN THE U. S. A.

CONTENTS

HOME-MADE BRANDIES

BRANDIES

1. APPLE BRANDY

Take seven gallons of water and boil one-half, putting the other into a barrel; add the boiling water to the cold, with one-half gallon of molasses and a little yeast. Keep the bung-hole open until fermentation ceases.

<><><>

2. OLD APPLE BRANDY

One gallon of neutral spirits, one-half cup of decoction of tea, one and one-half pints of alcoholic solution of starch, one-eighth ounce of sulphuric acid. This is flavored with one-fourth ounce of the oil of apples. Color with one ounce of sugar coloring.

<><><>

3. BLACKBERRY BRANDY

One-quarter pound essence of blackberry, one quart blackberry juice, one-quarter pound of gum arabic, one small barrel pure spirits.

9

4. CARAWAY BRANDY

Steep one ounce of caraway-seed and six ounces of loaf sugar with one quart of brandy. Let it stand nine days and then draw off.

◇—◇—◇

5. BLACK CHERRY BRANDY

Stone two pounds of black cherries and put on them one quart of brandy. Bruise the stones in a mortar, and then add them to the brandy. Cover them close and let them stand a month or six weeks. Then pour it clear from the sediment and bottle it. Morello cherries, managed in this way, make a fine cordial.

◇—◇—◇

6. CHERRY BRANDY

For this purpose use either morello cherries or small black cherries. Pick them from the stalks; fill the bottles nearly up to the necks, then fill up with brandy (some people use whiskey, gin, or spirit distilled from the lees of the wine.) In three weeks or a month strain off the spirit; to each quart add one pound of loaf sugar clarified, and flavor with tincture of cinnamon or cloves.

◇—◇—◇

7. ORANGE BRANDY

Put the chips of six Seville oranges in one quart of brandy, and let them steep a fortnight in a stone bottle close stopped. Boil two and two-thirds pints of spring water with eight ounces of the finest sugar, nearly an hour, very gently. Clarify the water and sugar with the white of an egg; then strain it through a jelly-bag, and boil it nearly half away. When it is cold, strain the brandy into the syrup.

❖❖❖

8. RASPBERRY BRANDY

Raspberry brandy is infused nearly after the same manner as cherry brandy, and drawn off with about the same addition of brandy to what is drawn off from the first, second, and third infusion, and dulcified accordingly, first making it of a bright deep color, omitting cinnamon and cloves in the first, but not in the second and third infusion. The second infusion will be somewhat paler than the first, and must be lightened in color by adding one pint cherry brandy, with five or more gallons of raspberry brandy, and the third infusion will require more cherry brandy to color it. It may be flavored with the juice of elderberry.

❖❖❖

9. HOW TO PREPARE ESSENCE OF COGNAC

Take 1 ounce oil cognac—the green oil is the best; put it in ½ gallon 95 per cent spirits. Cork it up tight, shake it frequently for about 3 days; then add 2 ounces strong ammonia. Let it stand 3 days longer; then place in a stone jar that will contain about 3 gallons, 1 pound fine black tea, 2 pounds prunes, having first mashed the prunes and broken the kernels. Pour on them 1 gallon spirits 20 above proof. Cover it close, and let it stand 8 days. Filter the liquor, and mix with that containing the oil and ammonia. Bottle it for use. This makes the best flavoring known for manufacturing brandies, or for adding to such cordials, syrups, etc., as require a fine brandy flavor.

<><><>

10. IMITATION COGNAC BRANDY

To 36 gallons French proof spirits, add 4 gallons Pellevoisin or Marette cognac, ½ gallon best sherry or Madeira wine, and 20 drops oil of cognac, dissolved in a little 95 per cent alcohol. Then pour 2 quarts boiling water over 2 ounces black tea; when cold, filter through flannel, and add a little maraschino; mix this with the other ingredients, and color the whole to suit, with caramel.

Another excellent formula is as follows: Dissolve 20 drops oil of cognac and 15 drops oil of bitter almonds in a little 95 per cent alcohol; add it to 40 gallons 60 per cent French spirit, with 2 pints tincture of raisin, 2 pints of tincture of prunes, 3 pints best Jamaica rum, 3 pints best sherry wine, and ½ ounce acetic ether. Color with caramel.

<><><>

11. IMITATION BRANDY

Take 40 gallons French spirit; add to it 1 pint tincture of raisins, 1 quart prune flavoring, ½ gallon best sherry or Madeira wine, and 1 pint wine vinegar. Then add 1 drachm oil of cognac, 12 drops oil of bitter almonds, ⅛ to ½ drachm tannin powder, each dissolved separately in 95 per cent alcohol. Color to suit with caramel.

---

12. IMITATION FRENCH BRANDY

To 40 gallons French proof spirit, add 1 quart tincture of orris root, 1 pint vanilla flavoring, ½ gallon best sherry or Madeira wine, and 1 pint wine vinegar. Dissolve separately, 1 drachm oil of cognac and 12 drops oil of bitter almonds, each in a little 95 per cent alcohol, and add them to the mixture, coloring the whole to suit with caramel.

---

13. IMITATION PALE BRANDY

Infuse 1 drachm star-anise (breaking the star only) for 8 hours in ½ pint 95 per cent alcohol, and filter; add this to 40 gallons proof spirits; then add ½ gallon best Jamaica rum, and 1 pint of the best raspberry syrup. Dissolve 1 drachm oil of cognac, and 12 drops oil of bitter almonds, separately, in a little 95 per cent alcohol and mix them with the whole.

14. BLACKBERRY BRANDY

To 10 gallons blackberry juice and 25 gallons spirits 40 above proof, add 1 drachm each of oil of cloves and oil of cinnamon dissolved in 95 per cent alcohol, and 12 pounds white sugar dissolved in 6 gallons water. Dissolve the oils separately in ½ pint 95 per cent alcohol; mix both together and use one half the quantity; if the cordial is not sufficiently flavored, use the balance.

15. BLACKBERRY BRANDY

¼ ounce each of cinnamon, cloves and mace, 1 drachm cardamon. Grind to a coarse powder; add to 16 pounds of blackberries, mashed and 5 gallons of 95 per cent alcohol. Macerate for two weeks; press it; then add 10 pounds of sugar, dissolved in 3⅜ gallons of water. Filter.

16. CHERRY BRANDY

Mash 16 pounds of black cherries with their stones; 5 gallons 95 per cent alcohol. Macerate for two weeks; press it; then add 10 pounds of sugar, dissolved in 3⅜ gallons of water. Filter.

17. PEACH BRANDY

Mash 18 pounds of peaches with their stones; macerate them for 24 hours with 4¾ gallons of 95 per cent alcohol and 4 gallons water. Strain, press and filter; add 5 pints white plain syrup. Color dark yellow with burnt sugar coloring.

HOME-MADE CORDIALS

CORDIALS

To filter cordials, cover the bottom of a sieve with clean blotting-paper. Pour the liquor into it (having set a vessel underneath to receive it), and let drip through the paper and through the sieve. Renew the paper frequently and fasten it down with pins. This process is slow, but makes the liquor beautifully clear.

◇◇◇

18. ANISE-SEED CORDIAL

Take ½ pound bruised anise-seed, 3 gallons proof spirit, 1 quart of water. Draw off two gallons with a moderate fire. This water should never be reduced below proof, because the large quantity of oil with which it is impregnated will render it milky and foul when brought down below proof. But if there is a necessity for doing this the transparency may be restored by filtration.

◇◇◇

19. BLACKBERRY CORDIAL

Mash and strain the berries through sieve. To 1 gallon of juice put 1 pound of sugar. Boil and add 1 tablespoon of allspice, 1 tablespoon of cloves. Cook till thick. When nearly cold add one quart of whiskey or brandy. Bottle and seal.

◇–◇–◇

20. CARAWAY CORDIAL

Take 1 teaspoonful of oil of caraway, four drops of cassia-lignea oil, 1 drop of essence of orange peel, 1 drop of essence of lemon, 5 quarts and a gill of spirits, 1¾ pounds of loaf sugar. Make it up and fine it down.

◇–◇–◇

21. CITRON CORDIAL

½ pound yellow rind of citrons, 2 ounces orange peel, ⅓ ounce bruised nutmegs, 2⅙ gallons proof spirit; macerate, add water sufficient, and ½ pound of fine lump sugar for every gallon of the cordial.

◇–◇–◇

22. CLOVE CORDIAL

Take ¼ of a pound of cloves, bruised, 1 ounce pimento, or allspice, 2 gallons proof spirit. Digest the mixture 12 hours in a gentle heat, and then draw off with a pretty brisk fire. The water may be colored red, either by strong tincture of cochineal, alkanet or corn poppy-flowers. It may be dulcified at pleasure with refined sugar.

23. CORIANDER CORDIAL

⅓ pound coriander seeds, ⅓ ounce of caraways, and the peel and juice of ½ orange to every gallon of proof spirit.

◇—◇—◇

24. GINGER CORDIAL

Pick 1 pound of large white currants from their stalks, lay them in a basin, and strew over them the rind of an orange and a lemon cut very thin, or ½ teaspoonful of essence of lemon, and 1 ounce and one-half of the best ground ginger, and 1 quart of good whiskey. Let all lie for 24 hours. If it tastes strong of the ginger, then strain it; if not, let it lie for 12 hours longer. To every quart of strained juice add 1 pound of loaf sugar pounded. When the sugar is quite dissolved, and the liquor appears clear, bottle it. This cordial is also extremely good made with raspberries instead of currants.

◇—◇—◇

25. LEMON CORDIAL

Pare off very thin the yellow rind of some fine lemons. Cut the lemons in half and squeeze out the juice. To each pint of the juice allow ½ pound of loaf sugar. Mix the juice, the peel, and the sugar together. Cover it and let it set 24 hours. Then mix it with an equal quantity of white brandy. Put it into a jug, and let it set a month. Then strain through a linen bag and afterward through blotting-paper before you bottle it.

26. LIME JUICE CORDIAL

Lime juice cordial that will keep good for any length of time may be made as follows: 6 pounds sugar, 4 pints water, 4 ounces citric acid, ½ ounce boric acid. Dissolve by the aid of a gentle heat, and when cold add 60 ounces refined lime juice, 4 ounces tincture of lemon peel, water to make up 2 gallons.

---

27. STRAWBERRY OR RASPBERRY CORDIAL

Sugar down the berries overnight, using more sugar than you would for the table, about half as much again. In the morning lay them in a hair sieve over the basin; let them remain until evening, so as to thoroughly drain. Then put the juice in a thick flannel bag; let it drain all night, being careful not to squeeze it, as that takes out the brightness and clearness. All this should be done in a cool cellar, or it will be apt to sour. Add brandy in the proportion of ⅓ the quantity of juice, and as much more sugar as the taste demands. Bottle it tightly. It will keep 6 to 8 years, and is better at last than at first.

---

28. WHISKEY CORDIAL

Take 1 ounce of cinnamon, 1 ounce of ginger, 1 ounce of coriander seed, ½ ounce of mace, ½ ounce of cloves, ½ ounce of cubebs. Add 3 gallons of proof spirit and 2½ quarts of water. Now tie up 1⅓ ounces of English saffron, 1 pound of raisins (stoned), 1 pound dates; 3 ounces licorice root. Let these stand 12 hours in 2½ quarts of water; strain, and add it to the above. Dulcify the whole with fine sugar.

⟞⟝

29. ANISETTE DE BOURDEAUX

Take 9 ounces sugar, 6 drops aniseed. Rub them together and add, by degrees, 2 pints spirits of wine, 4 pints water. Filter.

⟞⟝

30. CREME DES BARBADOES

Take 1 dozen middling sized lemons, 3 large citrons, 14 pounds loaf sugar, ¼ pound fresh balm leaves, 5 quarts spirits of wine, 7 quarts of water. Cut lemons and citrons in thin slices and put them into a cask, pour upon them the spirit of wine, bung down close, and let it stand 10 days or a fortnight; then break the sugar, and boil it for ½ hour in the water, skimming it frequently. Then chop the balm leaves, put them into a large pan, and pour upon them the boiling liquor, and let it stand till quite cold; then strain it through a lawn sieve, and put it to the spirits, etc., in the cask. Bung down close, and in a fortnight draw it off. Strain it through a jelly-bag and let remain to fine; then bottle it.

31. CREME DE NOYAU DE MARTINIQUE

Take 20 pounds of loaf sugar, 3 gallons of spirit of wine, 3 pints of orange-flower water, 1¼ pounds of bitter almonds, 2 drams of essence of lemon, 4½ gallons of water. The produce will exceed 8 gallons. Put 2 pounds of the loaf sugar into a jug or can, pour upon it the essence of lemon, and 1 quart of the spirit of wine. Stir till the sugar is dissolved, and the essence completely incorporated. Bruise the almonds and put them into a 4 gallon stone bottle or cask, add the remainder of the spirit of wine, and the mixture from the jug or can. Let it stand a week or ten days, shaking it frequently. Then add the remainder of the sugar, and boil it in the 4½ gallons of water for ¾ of an hour, taking off the scum as it rises. When cold, put in a cask; add the spirit, almonds, etc., from the stone bottle, and lastly the orange-water. Bung it down close and let it stand 3 weeks or a month; then strain it off in a jelly-bag, and when fine, bottle it off. When the pink is wanted, add cochineal, in powder, at the rate of ½ dram or two scruples to 1 quart.

❖

32. CREME D'ORANGE OF SUPERIOR FLAVOR

Take 1 dozen middling sized oranges, 1¼ pints orange-flower water, 6 pounds loaf sugar, 2⅔ quarts spirit of wine, ½ ounce tincture of saffron, 4⅔ quarts water. Cut the oranges in slices, put them in a cask, add the spirit and orange-flower water, let it stand a fortnight. Then boil the sugar in the water for ½ hour, pour it out, and let it stand till cold; then add it to the mixture in the cask; and put in the tincture of saffron. Let it remain a fortnight longer; then strain, and proceed as directed in the recipe for Creme de Barbadoes, and a very fine cordial will be produced.

❖❖❖

33. EAU DE BARBADOES

Take 1 ounce of fresh orange peel, 4 ounces of fresh lemon peel, 1 dram coriander, 4 pints proof spirit. Distill in a bath heat, and add white sugar in powder.

❖❖❖

34. EAU DE BIGARADE

Take the outer or yellow part of the peels of seven bigarades (a kind of orange), ¼ ounce of nutmegs, ⅛ ounce of mace, ½ gallon of fine proof spirit, 1 quart of water. Digest all these together two days in a close vessel, after which draw off a gallon with a gentle fire, and dulcify with fine sugar.

❖❖❖

35. EAU DEVINE

Take ½ gallon of spirit of wine, ½ dram essence of lemons and ½ dram essence of bergamot. Distill in a bath heat, add 2 pounds sugar, dissolved in 1 gallon of pure water, and lastly 2½ ounces of orange-flower water.

36. ELEPHANT'S MILK

Take 2 ounces gum benzoin, 1 pint spirit of wine, 2½ pints boiling water. When cold, strain and add 1½ pounds sugar.

<>-<>-<>

37. HUILE DE VENUS

Take 6 ounces of flowers of wild carrot, picked, 10 pints spirit of wine. Distill in a bath heat. To the spirit add as much syrup of Capillaire; it may be colored with cochineal.

<>-<>-<>

38. LIGNODELLA

Take the thin peel of 3 oranges and 3 lemons; steep them in ½ gallon of brandy or rum, close stopped for 2 or 3 days. Then take 3 quarts of water and 1½ pounds of loaf sugar clarified with the whites of 2 eggs. Let it boil ¼ hour, then strain it through a fine sieve, and let it stand till cold; strain the brandy with the peels, add the juice of 3 oranges and 5 lemons to each gallon. Keep it close stopped up 5 weeks, then bottle it.

<>-<>-<>

39. MARASCHINO

1 gallon proof whiskey, 2 quarts of water, dissolve 4 pounds of sugar, ⅓ dram oil of bergamot, ⅓ dram oil

of cloves, 2 drops oil of cinnamon, ⅔ ounce of nutmegs, bruised, 5 ounces of orange peel, 1 ounce of bitter almonds, bruised, ⅓ dram oil of lemon. Dissolve the oil in alcohol; color with cochineal and burnt sugar.

❖❖❖

40. MARASQUIN DE GROSEILLES

Take 8½ pounds of gooseberries, quite ripe, 1 pound black cherry leaves. Bruise and ferment; distill and rectify the spirits. To each pint of this spirit add as much distilled water, and 1 pound of sugar.

❖❖❖

41. NECTAR

Take 3 gallons of red ratafia, ¼ ounce of cassia-oil, and an equal quantity of the oil of caraway seeds. Dissolve in a little spirit of wine, and make up with orange wine so as to fill up the jug. Sweeten, if wanted, by adding a small lump of sugar in the glass.

❖❖❖

42. NOYAU

Take 1½ gallons of French brandy, 1 in 5, 6 ounces of the best French prunes, 2 ounces of celery, 3 ounces of the kernels of apricots, nectarines, and peaches, and 1 ounce of bitter almonds, all gently bruised, 2 pennyweights of essence of lemon peel, 1½ pounds of loaf sugar. Let the whole stand 10 days or a fortnight. Then draw off, and add to the clear noyau as much rose-water as will make up to 2 gallons.

———◇◆◇———

43. RATAFIA

This is a liquor prepared from different kinds of fruits, and is of different colors, according to the fruits made use of. These fruits should be gathered when in their greatest perfection, and the largest and most beautiful of them chosen for the purpose. The following is the method for making red ratafia, fine and soft: Take 12 pounds of the black-heart cherries, 2 pounds black cherries, 1½ pounds raspberries, 1½ pounds strawberries. Pick the fruit from their stalks, and bruise them, in which state let them continue 12 hours; then press out the juice, and to every pint of it add ½ pound of sugar. When the sugar is dissolved, run the whole through the filtering-bag, and add to it 3 pints of proof spirit. Then take 2 ounces of cinnamon, 2 ounces mace, 1 dram cloves. Bruise these spices, put them into an alembic with ½ gallon of proof spirit and 1 quart of water, and draw off a gallon with a brisk fire. Add as much of the spicy spirit to the red ratafia as will render it agreeable; about ¼ is the usual proportion.

———◇◆◇———

44. RATAFIA NO. 2

Ratafia may be made with the juice of any fruit. Take 6 quarts cherry juice and 2 pounds sugar, which you dissolve in the juice. Steep in 5 quarts brandy 10 days. 1 dram cinnamon, 12 cloves, 8 ounces peach leaves, 4 ounces bruised cherry kernels. Filter, mix both liquids, and filter again.

◇–◇–◇

45. RATAFIA NO. 3

Take 4 ounces of nutmegs, 5 pounds of bitter almonds, 9 pounds Lisbon sugar, 5 grains ambergris. Infuse these ingredients 3 days in 5 gallons of proof spirit, and filter it through a flannel bag for use. The nutmegs and bitter almonds must be bruised, and the ambergris rubbed with the Lisbon sugar in a marble mortar, before they are infused in the spirit.

◇–◇–◇

46. RATAFIA D'ANGELIQUE

Take ½ dram of angelica seed, 2 ounces stalks of angelica, 2 ounces bitter almonds, blanched, 6 pints proof spirit, 1 pound white sugar. Digest, strain and filter.

◇–◇–◇

47. RATAFIA DE BRON DE NOIX

Take 60 young walnuts whose shells are not yet hardened, 4 pints brandy, 12 ounces sugar, 15 grains mace, 15 grains cinnamon, 15 grains cloves. Digest for 2 to 3 months, press out the liquor, filter and keep it for 2 to 3 years.

48. RATAFIA DE CAFE

Take ½ pound of roasted coffee, ground, 2 quarts proof spirit, 10 ounces sugar. Digest for a week.

◇◇◇

49. RATAFIA DE CASSIS

Take 3 pounds of ripe black currants, ¼ dram cloves, ¼ dram cinnamon, 9 pints proof spirit, 1¾ pounds sugar. Digest for a fortnight.

◇◇◇

50. RATAFIA DES CERISES

Take 4 pounds morello cherries, with their kernels bruised, 4 pints proof spirit. Digest for a month, strain with expression, and then add ¾ pound of sugar.

◇◇◇

51. RATAFIA DE CHOCOLAT

Take 1 ounce Curaçoa cocoanuts rosted, ½ pound West India cocoanuts, roasted, 1 gallon proof spirit. Digest for a fortnight, strain, and then add 1½ pounds sugar, 30 drops tincture of vanilla.

◇◇◇

52. DRY OR SHARP RATAFIA

Take 15 pounds of cherries, 15 pounds of gooseberries, 3½ pounds mulberries, 5 pounds raspberries. Pick all these fruits clean from their stalks, etc., bruise them, and let them stand 12 hours, but do not suffer them to ferment. Press out the juice, and to every pint add 3 ounces of sugar. When the sugar is dissolved, run it through the filtering-bag, and to every 5 pints of liquor add 4 pints of proof spirit, together with the same proportion of spirit drawn from spices.

⬥⬥⬥

53. RATAFIA DE GRENOBER

Take 2 pounds of small wild black cherries, with their kernels bruised, 1 gallon proof spirit. Digest for a month, strain, and add 2 pounds of sugar. A little citron peel may also be added at pleasure.

⬥⬥⬥

54. RATAFIA DE NOYAU

Take of peach or apricot kernels, with their shells bruised, in number 120, 4 pints proof spirit, 10 ounces sugar. Some reduce the spirit of wine to proof with the juice of apricots or peaches, to make the liquor.

⬥⬥⬥

55. RATAFIA D'ECORCES D'ORANGES

Take 2 ounces of fresh peel of Seville oranges, ½ gallon proof spirit, ½ pound sugar. Digest for 6 hours.

56 RATAFIA DE THURO D'ORANGE

Take 2 pounds of fresh flowers of orange-tree, 1 gallon proof spirit, 1½ pounds of sugar. Digest for 6 hours.

❖❖❖

57. RATAFIA A LA VIOLETTE

Take 2 drams Florentine orris root, 1 ounce archil, 4 pints spirit of wine. Digest, strain, and add 4 pounds sugar.

❖❖❖

58. USQUEBAUGH, NO. 1

Usquebaugh is a strong compound liquor, chiefly taken by the dram. It is made in the highest perfection at Drogheda in Ireland. The following are the ingredients: Take 2 quarts of best brandy, ½ pound raisins, stoned, ½ ounce nutmegs, ½ ounce cardamoms, ¼ ounce saffron, rind of ½ Seville orange, ½ pound brown sugar candy. Shake these well every day for at least 14 days, and it will at the expiration of that time be ready to be fined for use.

❖❖❖

59. GENERAL DIRECTIONS FOR MAKING CORDIALS

The materials employed in the preparation of cordials are rain or distilled water, white sugar and clean, perfectly flavorless spirit. To these may be added the substances from which the flavor and aroma are extracted, which distinguish and give character to the particular cordial to be made, and also the articles employed as "finings" when artificial clarification is had recourse to. In the preparation or compounding of cordials, one of the first objects which engages the operator's attention is the production of an alcoholic solution of the aromatic principles which are to give them their peculiar aroma and flavor. This is done either by simple infusion or maceration, or by maceration and subsequent distillation, or by flavoring the spirit with essential oils. In the preparation of liqueurs, glycerine has been found to be admirably adapted for preserving the characteristic flavors of those compounds, and it has consequently become the great favorite of this class of manufactures.

<><><>

60. ANISETTE

To 30 gallons French proof spirit add 4 ounces essence of star anise dissolved in 95 per cent alcohol and 105 gallons syrup of 10° Baume. Stir for ½ an hour, settle and filter.

<><><>

61. CHAMPION ANISETTE

Put into a barrel 30 gallons 85 per cent alcohol. Add 4 ounces essence of anise seed, which dissolve in 2 gallons 95 per cent. alcohol. Add 103 gallons sugar syrup 10° Baume. Stir 15 minutes and let it rest 4 or 5 days, then filter. Add 2 or 3 sheets of filtering paper.

---

62. ANISE SEED CORDIAL

Dissolve 3 drachms of oil of anise seed in 2¾ gallons of 95 per cent alcohol; then add 2½ gallons of fine white syrup, mixed with 4¾ gallons of water. Stir and filter.

---

63. CARAWAY CORDIAL

Dissolve 6 drachms oil of caraway in 3 gallons 95 per cent alcohol; add a syrup made of 42 pounds of sugar and 4¾ gallons of water. Filter.

---

64. CORDIALS BY DISTILLATION

The solid ingredients should be coarsely pounded or bruised before digestion in the spirit, and this should be done immediately before putting them into the cask or vat; as, after they are bruised, they rapidly lose their aromatic properties by exposure to the air. The practice of drying the ingredients before pounding them, adopted by some workmen for the mere sake of lessening the labor, cannot be too much avoided, as the least exposure to heat tends to lessen their aromatic properties, which are very volatile. The length of time the ingredients should be digested in the spirit should never be less than 3 or 4 days, but a longer period is preferable when distillation is not employed. In either case the time allowed for digestion may be advantageously extended to 10 or 15 days, and frequent agitation should be had recourse to.

⟨><>

65. TO MAKE ABSINTHE

Put the following ingredients into a cask:—1½ pounds large absinthe, 2 pounds small absinthe, 2½ pounds long fennel, 2½ pounds star anise (breaking the star only), 2½ pounds green anise seed, 6 ounces coriander seed, and 1 pound hyssop; moisten the whole with a little water, allowing it time to soften and swell; then add 12 gallons 95 per cent alcohol, and steep for 2 or 3 days. Color the product, by steeping in it for 10 or 15 days ½ pound mint leaves, ¼ pound melissa leaves, ½ pound small absinthe, 2 ounces citron peel, and ½ pound bruised liquorice root. Strain and filter.

⟨><>

66. FINING WITH ISINGLASS FOR CORDIALS

Take half an ounce of the best isinglass, and dissolve it over a gentle fire, in a pint of water slightly seasoned with good vinegar, or three teaspoonfuls of lemon juice. Beat it from time to time, adding a little of the seasoned water. When you obtain a complete solution, gradually add the foaming liquid to the cordial, stirring all the while. Then stir for 15 minutes after it is all added, and let it rest for 3 days; by that time the cordial will be bright and clear. The above quantity is sufficient to clarify 25 gallons of cordial.

<><><>

67. TO MAKE SYRUPS FOR THE MANUFACTURE OF CORDIALS & LIQUORS

Take 1 pint of water to every 2 pounds of sugar used; this proportion will make a fine syrup, about 32° Baume, but the manufacturer often requires weaker syrups when preparing inferior cordials, and the easiest method of ascertaining the proper point of concentration is by the use of that variety of Baume's hydrometer, called a saccharometer. Beat up the whites of 2 eggs (if you are clarifying about 10 pounds of sugar, or mix in this proportion) until it is very frothy, and then mix in with the rest.

<><><>

68. KING'S CORDIAL

Dissolve in ½ pint of proof spirits, 1½ drachms each of the oils of caraway and cinnamon; extract the stones from 3 pounds of black cherries, and mash the fruit in a pan; grate 1 nutmeg; take 2 quarts of Madeira wine, 2 quarts of brandy, and 1 gallon of syrup; mix all together, and color with red saunders wood.

69. BLACKBERRY CORDIAL

To 1 quart blackberry juice, add 1 pound white sugar, 1 tablespoonful each cloves, allspice, cinnamon and nutmeg. Boil all together 15 minutes, add a wine-glass of whiskey, brandy or rum. Bottle while hot, cork tight and seal. This is almost a specific in diarrhea. Dose is 1 wine-glassful for an adult, half that quantity for a child; will often cure diarrhea. It can be taken 3 or 4 times a day if the case is severe.

HOME-MADE GIN

GIN

70. IMITATION SCHIEDAM GIN

Dissolve 3½ drachms oil of juniper in sufficient 95 per cent alcohol to make a clear liquid; add it to 40 gallons French spirits 10 above proof, with 8 ounces orange peel flavoring, 1 quart syrup, and 30 drops oil of sweet fennel.

◇—◇—◇

71. IMITATION OLD TOM LONDON GIN

Dissolve in 1 quart 95 per cent alcohol, 1 drachm oil of coriander, 1 drachm oil of cedar, ½ drachm oil of bitter almonds, ½ drachm oil of angelica, and ½ drachm oil of sweet fennel; add it to 40 gallons French spirit 10 above proof, with 1 pint orange-flower water, 1 quart syrup and 1 drachm oil of juniper dissolved in sufficient 95 per cent alcohol to be clear.

◇—◇—◇

72. TO CLARIFY GIN OR CORDIALS

Pulverize 1 pound ordinary crystals of alum, divide into 12 equal portions, and put up in blue papers marked No. 1. Next take 6 ounces carbonate (the ordinary sesquicarbonate) of soda, divide it into 12 parts and put them up in white papers marked No. 2. In place of the 6 ounces of carbonate of soda, 4 ounces dry salt of tartar may be substituted, but the white papers containing this latter substance must be kept in a dry, well corked bottle or jar. To clarify 30 to 36 gallons gin, dissolve the contents of one of the blue papers, as prepared above in about a pint of hot water, and stir it into the liquor thoroughly. Then dissolve the contents of one of the white papers in about ½ pint hot water, and stir well into the liquor; bung the cask close, and let the whole remain till the next day.

◇—◇—◇

73. TO BLANCH GIN OR OTHER WHITE LIQUOR

By using double the quantity of finings, that is, 2 of each of the powders as laid down in the foregoing receipt, the liquor will be blanched as well as clarified. It is well to recollect, however, that the more finings are employed, the greater the risk of injuring the liquor, which may have a tendency to become flat when "on draught."

◇—◇—◇

74. FININGS FOR GIN

To 100 gallons gin, take 4 ounces roche alum, and put it into 1 pint of pure water; boil it until it is dissolved, then gradually add 4 ounces salts of tartar; when nearly cold, put it into the gin, and stir it well with a staff for 10 minutes. The liquor must not be covered until it is fine; when this is accomplished, cover it up tight to prevent it from losing its strength.

75. TO REMOVE THE BLACKNESS FROM GIN

Some gin has a particular blackness; to remove which, take 1 ounce pulverized chalk and 2 or 3 ounces isinglass, dissolved; put this into the gin and it will become transparent. The above is enough for 50 gallons. The blackness which gin sometimes contracts by coming in contact with iron, may also be carried down by putting a solution of 2 ounces isinglass and 1 quart skimmed milk into the spirit.

HOW TO MIX ALL KINDS

OF

HOME-MADE

PLAIN AND FANCY DRINKS

Containing clear and reliable directions for mixing all
the beverages used in the United States together
with the most popular British, German, Italian, Russian, and Spanish recipes; em-
bracing punches, juleps, cobblers
etc., in endless variety.

MIXED DRINKS

76. BRANDY COCKTAIL

(Use small bar-glass)
Take 3 or 4 dashes of gum syrup
2 dashes of bitters (Boker's or Angostura)
1 wine-glass of brandy
1 or 2 dashes of Curaçoa
Fill the glass one-third full of shaved ice, shake up well and strain into a cocktail glass. Twist a small piece of lemon rind in it and serve.

<><><>

78. IMPROVED BRANDY COCKTAIL

(Use small bar-glass)
Take 2 dashes Boker's or Angostura Bitters
2 dashes Maraschino
3 dashes gum syrup
1 dash Absinthe
1 small piece of the yellow rind of a lemon, twisted to express the oil
1 small wine-glass of brandy.
Fill the glass one-third full of shaved ice, shake well and strain into a fancy cocktail glass, put the lemon

47

peel in the glass and serve. The flavor is improved by moistening the edge of the cocktail glass with a piece of lemon.

◇◇◇

79. WHISKEY COCKTAIL

(Use small bar-glass)
Take 3 or 4 dashes of gum syrup
2 dashes of bitters (Boker's)
1 wine-glass of whiskey
Fill one-third full of fine ice; shake and strain in a fancy red wine-glass. Put in a piece of twisted lemon peel in the glass and serve.

◇◇◇

80. GIN COCKTAIL

(Use small bar-glass)
Take 3 or 4 dashes of gum syrup
2 dashes of bitters (Boker's)
1 wine-glass of Holland gin
1 or 2 dashes of Curaçoa
Fill the glass one-third full of shaved ice, and strain into a cocktail glass. Twist a small piece of lemon peel, place it in the glass and serve.

81. FANCY VERMOUTH COCKTAIL

(Use small bar-glass)

Take 2 dashes Angostura bitters

2 dashes Maraschino

1 wine-glass of Vermouth

1 quarter slice of lemon

Fill the glass one-quarter full of shaved ice, shake well and strain into a cocktail glass; garnish with the lemon.

◇◇◇

82. ABSINTHE COCKTAIL

(Use small bar-glass)

Take 2 dashes of Anisette

1 dash of Angostura bitters

1 pony-glass of Absinthe

Pour about one wine-glass of water into the tumbler in a small stream from the ice pitcher, or preferably from an absinthe glass. Shake up *very* thoroughly with ice, and strain into a claret glass.

◇◇◇

83. JAPANESE COCKTAIL

(Use small bar-glass)

Take 1 tablespoonful of orgeat syrup

2 dashes of Boker's bitters

1 wine-glass of brandy

1 or 2 pieces of lemon peel

Fill the tumbler one-third with ice, stir well with a spoon and strain into a cocktail glass.

84. JERSEY COCKTAIL

(Use large bar-glass)
Take 1 teaspoonful of fine white sugar
2 dashes of bitters
3 or 4 lumps of ice.
Fill tumbler with cider, and mix well with a spoon and re-move the ice before serving.

◇–◇–◇

85. MANHATTAN COCKTAIL

(Use small bar-glass)
Take 2 dashes of Curaçoa or Maraschino
1 pony of rye whiskey
1 wine-glass of Vermouth
3 dashes of Boker's bitters
2 small lumps of ice
Shake up well, and strain into a claret glass. Put a quarter of a slice of lemon in the glass and serve. If the customer prefers it very sweet use also two dashes of gum syrup.

◇–◇–◇

86. SARATOGA COCKTAIL

(Use small bar-glass)
Take 2 dashes Angostura bitters
1 pony of brandy
1 pony of whiskey
1 pony of vermouth
Shake up well with two small lumps of ice; strain into a claret glass, and serve with a quarter of a slice of lemon.

87. MARTINEZ COCKTAIL

(Use small bar-glass)
Take 1 dash of Boker's bitters
2 dashes of Maraschino
1 pony of Old Tom gin
1 wine-glass of vermouth
2 small lumps of ice

Shake up thoroughly, and strain into a large cocktail glass. Put a quarter of a slice of lemon in the glass and serve. If the guest prefers it very sweet add two dashes of gum syrup.

<><><>

88. WHISKEY DAISY

(Use small bar-glass)
Take 3 dashes gum syrup
2 dashes Orgeat syrup
The juice of half a small lemon
1 wine-glass of Bourbon, or rye whiskey

Fill one glass one-third full of shaved ice. Shake well, strain into a large cocktail glass, and fill up with Seltzer or Apollinaris water.

<><><>

89. GIN DAISY

(Use small-bar glass)
Take 3 or 4 dashes of orgeat, or gum syrup
3 dashes of Maraschino
The juice of half a small lemon
1 wine-glass of Holland gin

Fill glass one-third full of shaved ice. Shake well, strain into a large cocktail glass, and fill up with Seltzer or Apollinaris water.

❖❖❖

90. MINT JULEP

(Use large bar-glass)
Take 1 tablespoonful of white pulverized sugar
2½ tablespoonfuls of water, mix well with a spoon
1½ wine-glasses full of brandy

Take three or four sprigs of fresh mint, and press them well in the sugar and water, until the flavor of the mint is extracted; add the brandy, and fill the glass with fine shaved ice, then draw out the sprigs of mint and insert them in the ice with the stems downward, so that the leaves will be above, in the shape of a bouquet; arrange the berries, and small pieces of sliced orange on top in a tasty manner, dash with Jamaica rum, and serve with a straw.

❖❖❖

91. GIN JULEP

(Use large bar-glass)
The gin julep is made with the same ingredients as the mint julep, omitting the fancy fixings.

92. WHISKEY JULEP

(Use large bar-glass)
The whiskey julep is made the same as the mint julep, omitting all fruits and berries.

◇◇◇

93. PINEAPPLE JULEP

(For a party of five)
Take the juice of two oranges
1 gill of rasperry syrup
1 gill of Maraschino
1 gill of Old Tom gin
1 quart bottle Sparkling Moselle
1 ripe pineapple, peeled, sliced and cut up
Put all the materials in a glass bowl; ice, and serve in flat glasses ornamented with berries in season.

◇◇◇

94. BRANDY SMASH

(Use small bar-glass)
Take 1 teaspoonful of white sugar
2 tablespoonfuls of water
3 or 4 sprigs of tender mint
1 wine-glass full of brandy
Press the mint in the sugar and water to extract the flavor, add the brandy, and fill the glass two-thirds full of shaved ice. Stir thoroughly and ornament with half a slice of orange, and a few fresh sprigs of mint. Serve with a straw.

95. GIN SMASH

(Use small bar-glass)
Take 1 teaspoonful of fine white sugar
2 teaspoonfuls of water
1 wine-glass of gin
3 or 4 sprigs of tender mint

Put the mint in the glass, then the sugar and water. Mash the mint to extract the flavor, add the gin, and fill up the glass with shaved ice. Stir up well, and ornament with two or three fresh sprigs of mint.

96. WHISKEY SMASH

(Use small bar-glass)
Take 1 teaspoonful of fine white sugar
2 teaspoonfuls of water
3 or 4 sprigs of young mint
1 wine-glass of whiskey

Proceed exactly as directed in the last recipe

97. BRANDY FIX

(Use small bar-glass)
Take 1 large teaspoonful of fine white sugar dissolved in a little water

The juice of a quarter of a lemon
3 dashes of Curaçoa
1 wine-glass of brandy

Fill the glass two-thirds full of shaved ice. Stir well and ornament the top with slices of lemon or lime.

98. GIN FIX

(Use small bar-glass)

Take 1 large teaspoonful of powdered white sugar
　dissolved in a little water

2 dashes of Raspberry syrup

The juice of a quarter of a lemon

1 wine-glass of Holland gin

Fill up the glass two-thirds full of shaved ice, stir thoroughly, and ornament the top with berries in season. Old Tom gin may be used if preferred.

<><><>

99. WHISKEY FIX

(Use small bar-glass)

Take 1 large teaspoonful of powdered white sugar,
　dissolved in a little water

The juice of half a lemon

1 wine-glass of Bourbon or rye whiskey

Fill up the glass about two-thirds full of shaved ice, stir well, and ornament the top of the glass as directed in the last recipe.

<><><>

100. SHERRY COBBLER

(Use large bar-glass)

Take 1 tablespoonful of fine white sugar

1 slice of orange, cut up into quarters

2 small pieces of pineapple

Fill the glass nearly full of shaved ice, then fill it up with sherry wine. Shake up, ornament the top with berries in season, and serve with a straw.

101. CHAMPAGNE COBBLER

(use bottle of wine to four large bar-glasses)
Take 1 teaspoonful of sugar
1 piece each of orange and lemon peel
Fill the tumbler one-third full of shaved ice, and fill balance with wine, ornament in a tasty manner with berries in season. Serve with straws.

⬦⬦⬦

102. CATAWBA COBBLER

(Use small bar-glass)
Take 1 teaspoonful of fine white sugar, dissolved in a little water
1 slice of orange cut into quarters
Fill the glass half full of shaved ice, then fill it up with Catawba wine. Ornament the top with berries in season, and serve with a straw.

⬦⬦⬦

103. CLARET COBBLER

(Use large bar-glass)
This drink is made the same way as the Catawba cobbler, using Claret wine instead of Catawba.

⬦⬦⬦

104. SAUTERNE COBBLER

(Use large bar-glass)
This is the same as Catawba cobbler, using Sauterne instead of a Catawba.

105. WHISKEY COBBLER

Take 1½ wine-glass of whiskey

1 teaspoonful of white sugar dissolved in a little water

1 slice of orange cut into quarters

1 dash of Maraschino

Fill the tumbler with shaved ice, shake up thoroughly, ornament with berries, and serve with a straw.

<><><>

106. GIN SOUR

(Use small bar-glass)

Take 1 large teaspoonful of white sugar dissolved in a little Seltzer or Apollinaris water

2 or 3 dashes of lemon juice

1 wine-glass of Holland or Old Tom gin

Fill the glass full of shaved ice, shake up, and strain into a claret glass. Dress the top with orange, or pineapple and berries

<><><>

107. WHISKEY SOUR

(Use small bar-glass)

Take 1 large teaspoonful of powdered white sugar, dissolved in a little Seltzer or Apollinaris water

The juice of half a small lemon

1 wine-glass of Bourbon or rye whiskey

Fill the glass full of shaved ice, shake up and strain into a claret glass. Ornament with berries.

108. BRANDY SOUR

(Use small bar-glass)
Take 1 large teaspoonful of powdered white sugar,
    dissolved in a little Apollinaris or Seltzer water
The juice of half a lemon
1 dash of Curaçoa
1 wine-glass of Brandy
Fill the glass with shaved ice, shake, and strain into a
claret glass. Ornament with orange and berries.

<><><>

109. EGG SOUR

(Use small bar-glass)
Take 1 teaspoonful of powdered white sugar
3 dashes of lemon juice
1 pony of Curaçoa
1 pony of brandy
1 egg
2 or 3 small lumps of ice
Shake up well, and remove the ice before serving.

<><><>

110. APPLE TODDY

(Use medium bar-glass)
Take 1 large teaspoonful of fine white sugar dis-
    solved in a little boiling hot water
1 wine-glass of cider brandy (apple jack)
½ of a baked apple
Fill the glass two-thirds full of boiling water, stir up
and grate a little nutmeg on top. Serve with a spoon.

111. COLD BRANDY TODDY

(Use small bar-glass)
Take 1 teaspoonful of fine white sugar
½ wine-glass of water
1 wine-glass of brandy
1 lump of ice
Dissolve the sugar in the water, add the brandy and ice, stir with a spoon.

<><><>

112. HOT BRANDY TODDY

(Use small bar-glass)
Take 1 teaspoonful of fine white sugar
1 wine-glass of brandy
Dissolve the sugar in a little boiling water, add the brandy and pour boiling water into the glass until it is two-thirds full. Grate a little nutmeg on top.

<><><>

113. COLD GIN TODDY

(Use small bar-glass)
Take 1 teaspoonful of powdered white sugar
½ wine-glass of water
1 wine-glass of gin
1 lump of ice
Dissolve the sugar in the water, add the brandy and ice, and stir with a spoon.

114. HOT GIN TODDY

(Use small bar-glass)
Take 1 teaspoonful of powdered white sugar
1 wine-glass of Holland, or Old Tom gin (as pre-
     ferred)
Dissolve the sugar in boiling water, add the gin, and
pour boiling water into the glass until it is two-thirds
full.

◇◇◇

115. COLD WHISKEY TODDY

(Use small bar-glass)
Take 1 teaspoonful of fine white sugar
1 wine-glass of Bourbon, or rye whiskey
1 lump of ice
Dissolve the sugar in the water, add the whiskey and
ice, and stir with a spoon.

To make HOT WHISKEY TODDY, dissolve the
sugar in boiling water, omit the ice, and pour boiling
water into the glass, until it is two-thirds hot

◇◇◇

116. COLD IRISH WHISKEY TODDY

(Use small bar-glass)
Take 1 teaspoonful of fine white sugar
1 wine-glass of Kinahan's L.L. or Jamieson's
     whiskey
2 wine-glasses of water
1 lump of ice

Dissolve the sugar in the water, add the whiskey and ice, and stir with a spoon. This is a delicious drink if made with either of the above brands of whiskey, preferably the first.

❖❖❖

117. EGG NOGG

(Use large bar-glass)
Take 1 large teaspoonful of powdered white sugar
1 fresh egg
½ wine-glass of brandy
½ wine-glass of Santa Cruz rum
A little shaved ice

Fill the glass with rich milk and shake up the ingredients until they are thoroughly mixed. Pour the mixture into a goblet excluding the ice, and grate a little nutmeg on top. This may be made by using a wine-glass of either of the above liquors, instead of both combined. Every well ordered bar should have a tin egg-nogg "shaker," which is a great aid in mixing this beverage.

❖❖❖

118. HOT EGG NOGG

(Use large bar-glass)
This drink is very popular in California, and is made in precisely the same manner as the cold egg nogg above, except that you must use boiling water instead of ice.

119. SHERRY EGG NOGG

(Use large bar-glass)

Take 1½ teaspoonfuls of fine white sugar

1 fresh egg

2 or 3 lumps of ice

2 wine-glasses of Sherry wine

Fill the glass with rich milk, shake up until the egg is thoroughly mixed with the other ingredients. Strain the mixture into a large goblet, excluding the ice, and grate a little nutmeg on top.

---

120. GENERAL HARRISON'S EGG NOGG

(Use large bar-glass)

Take 1½ teaspoonfuls of sugar

1 fresh egg

2 or 3 small lumps of ice

Fill the tumbler with cider, and shake well

This is a delicious drink, and was very popular on the Mississippi River in old times. It is said to have been General Harrison's favorite beverage.

---

121. WHISKEY FIZZ

(Use medium bar-glass)

Take 1 teaspoonful of fine white sugar

1 small lump of ice

3 dashes of lemon juice

1 wine-glass of Bourbon or rye whiskey

Fill up the glass with Seltzer or Apollinaris water, stir thoroughly and serve.

122. BRANDY FIZZ

(Use medium bar-glass)
Take 1 teaspoonful of powdered white sugar
3 dashes of lemon juice
1 wine-glass of brandy
1 small lump of ice
Fill up the glass with Apollinaris or Seltzer water, stir thoroughly and serve.

<><><>

123. GIN FIZZ

(Use medium bar-glass)
Take 1 teaspoonful of powdered white sugar
3 dashes of lemon juice
1 wine-glass of Holland gin
1 small piece of ice
Fill up the glass with Apollinaris or Seltzer water, stir thoroughly and serve.

<><><>

124. SILVER FIZZ

(Use large bar-glass)
Take 1 tablespoonful of pulverized white sugar
3 dashes of lemon or lime juice
The white of one egg
1 wine-glass of Old Tom gin
2 or 3 small lumps of ice
Shake up thoroughly, strain into a medium bar-glass and fill it up with Seltzer water.

125. GOLDEN FIZZ

(Use large bar-glass)
Take 1 tablespoonful of fine white sugar
3 dashes of lemon or lime juice
The yolk of one egg
1 wine-glass of Old Tom gin
2 or 3 lumps of ice

Shake up thoroughly, strain into a medium bar-glass, and fill it up with Seltzer water.

<><><>

126. BRANDY SLING

(Use small bar-glass)
Take 1 small teaspoonful of powdered white sugar
1 wine-glass of water
1 small lump of ice
1 wine-glass of brandy

Dissolve the sugar in the water, add the brandy, and ice, stir well with a spoon. Grate a little nutmeg on top, and serve.

<><><>

127. GIN SLING

(Use small bar-glass)
Take 1 small teaspoonful of fine white sugar
1 wine-glass of water
1 wine-glass of brandy
1 small lump of ice

Dissolve the sugar in the water, add the brandy and ice, stir thoroughly with a spoon. Grate a little nutmeg on top and serve.

128. HOT GIN SLING

(Use medium bar-glass)
Take 1 small teaspoonful of powdered white sugar
1 wine-glass of Holland gin
Dissolve the sugar in a little boiling water, add the gin, fill the glass two-thirds full of boiling water. Grate a little nutmeg on top and serve.

❖❖❖

129. WHISKEY SLING

(Use small bar-glass)
Take 1 small teaspoonful of powdered white sugar
1 wine-glass of water
1 wine-glass of Bourbon or rye whiskey
Dissolve the sugar in the water, add the whiskey and ice, stir thoroughly with a spoon. Grate a little nutmeg on top, and serve.

❖❖❖

130. HOT WHISKEY SLING

(Use medium bar-glass)
Take 1 small teaspoonful of powdered sugar
1 wine-glass of Bourbon or rye whiskey
Dissolve the sugar in a little hot water, add the whiskey, and fill the glass two-thirds full of boiling water. Grate a little nutmeg on top, and serve.

131. HOT SPICED RUM

(Use medium bar-glass)

Take 1 small teaspoonful of powdered white sugar

1 wine-glass of Jamaica rum

1 teaspoonful of spices (allspice, and cloves not
    ground)

1 piece of sweet butter, as large as half a chestnut
Dissolve the sugar in a little boiling water, add the rum,
spices and butter, and fill the glass two-thirds full of
boiling water.

132. HOT RUM

(Use medium bar-glass)

Take 1 small teaspoonful of powdered sugar

1 wine-glass Jamaica rum

1 piece of sweet butter, as large as half a chestnut.
Dissolve the sugar in a little boiling water, add the rum
and butter, fill the glass two-thirds full of boiling water,
stir, grate a little nutmeg on top, and serve.

133. BLUE BLAZER

(Use two silver-plated mugs)

Take 1 small teaspoonful of powdered white sugar
    dissolved in 1 wine-glass of boiling water

1 wine-glass of Scotch whiskey
Put the whiskey and the boiling water in one mug, ignite
the liquid with fire, and while blazing mix both ingre-

dients by pouring them four or five times from one mug to the other. If well done this will have the appearance of a continued stream of liquid fire.

The novice in mixing this beverage should be careful not to scald himself. To become proficient in throwing the liquid from one mug to the other, it will be necessary to practise for some time with cold water.

◇—◇—◇

134. TOM AND JERRY

(Use punch-bowl for the mixture)
Take 12 fresh eggs
½ small bar-glass of Jamaica rum
1½ teaspoonfuls of ground cinnamon
½ teaspoonful of ground cloves
½ teaspoonful of ground allspice
Sufficient fine white sugar

Beat the whites of the eggs to a stiff froth and the yolks until they are thin as water, then mix together and add the spice and rum, stir up thoroughly, and thicken with sugar until the mixture attains the consistency of a light batter.

A larger or smaller quantity of this mixture may be made by increasing or diminishing the proportions of the ingredients given in the above recipe.

N.B.—A teaspoonful of cream of tartar, or about as much carbonate of soda as you can get on a dime, will prevent the sugar from settling to the bottom of the mixture.

135. HOW TO SERVE TOM AND JERRY

(Use small bar-glass)
Take 1 tablespoonful of the above mixture
1 wine-glass of brandy
Fill the glass with boiling water, grate a little nutmeg on top, and serve with a spoon.

Adepts at the bar, serving Tom and Jerry sometimes employ the following mixture:—one-half brandy, one-quarter Jamaica rum, one-quarter Santa Cruz rum. For convenience, these proportions are mixed and kept in a bottle, and a wine-glassful is used to each tumbler of Tom and Jerry, instead of brandy plain.

---

136. TOM COLLINS WHISKEY

(Use small bar-glass)
Take 5 or 6 dashes of gum syrup
Juice of a small lemon
1 large wine-glass of whiskey
2 or 3 lumps of ice
Shake up well and strain into a large bar-glass. Fill up the glass with plain soda water and imbibe while it is lively.

---

137. TOM COLLINS BRANDY

(Use large bar-glass)
The same as Tom Collins Whiskey, substituting brandy for whiskey.

138. TOM COLLINS GIN

(Use large bar-glass)

The same as Tom Collins Whiskey, substituting gin for whiskey.

◇◇◇

139. HOT BRANDY FLIP

(Use large bar-glass)

Take 1 teaspoonful of sugar

1 wine-glass of brandy

Yolk of one egg

Dissolve the sugar in a little hot water, add the brandy and egg, shake up thoroughly, pour into a medium bar-glass, and fill it one-half full of boiling water. Grate a little nutmeg on top, and serve.

◇◇◇

140. HOT RUM FLIP

(Use large bar-glass)

Same as Brandy Flip, substituting Jamaica rum instead of brandy.

◇◇◇

141. HOT WHISKEY FLIP

(Use large bar-glass)

Same as Brandy Flip, substituting whiskey instead of brandy.

142. HOT GIN FLIP

(Use large bar-glass)
Same as Brandy Flip, substituting Holland gin instead of brandy.

◇◇◇

143. COLD BRANDY FLIP

(Use large bar-glass)
Take 1 teaspoonful powdered sugar
1 wine-glass of brandy
½ wine-glass of water
1 fresh egg
2 lumps of ice
Dissolve the sugar in the water, add the brandy, egg and ice, shake up thoroughly, strain into a small bar-glass. Serve with a little nutmeg on top.

◇◇◇

144. COLD RUM FLIP

(Use large bar-glass)
Take one teaspoonful of powdered sugar, dissolved in
    a little water.
1 wine-glass of Jamaica rum
1 fresh egg
2 or 3 lumps of ice
Shake up thoroughly, strain in a medium glass, and grate a little nutmeg on top.

145. COLD GIN FLIP

(Use large bar-glass)
Same as Cold Rum Flip, substituting Holland gin instead of Jamaica rum.

❖❖❖

146. COLD WHISKEY FLIP

(Use large bar-glass)
Same as Rum Flip, substituting Bourbon or rye whiskey instead of Jamaica rum.

❖❖❖

147. PORT WINE FLIP

(Use large bar-glass)
Take 1 small teaspoonful of powdered white sugar
1 large wine-glass of port wine
1 fresh egg
2 or 3 small lumps of ice
Break the egg into the glass, add the sugar, and lastly the wine and ice. Shake up thoroughly and strain into a medium sized goblet.

❖❖❖

148. SHERRY WINE FLIP

(Use large bar-glass)
This is made precisely as the Port Wine Flip, substituting Sherry wine, instead of Port.

149. PORT WINE SANGAREE

(Use medium bar-glass)
Take 1 claret-glass of Port wine
½ teaspoonful of powdered white sugar
2 or 3 small lumps of ice
Shake up well, strain into a small bar-glass, and serve with a little grated nutmeg on top.

150. SHERRY SANGAREE

(Use medium bar-glass)
Take 1 claret glass of Sherry wine
½ teaspoonful of fine white sugar
2 or 3 small lumps of ice
Shake up well, strain into a small bar-glass, serve with a little grated nutmeg.

151. BRANDY SANGAREE

(Use medium bar-glass)
Take ½ teaspoonful of fine white sugar dissolved
    in a little water
1 wine-glass of brandy
Fill the glass one-third of shaved ice, shake up well, strain into a small glass and dash a little Port wine on top. Serve with a little grated nutmeg.

152. GIN SANGAREE

(Use medium bar-glass)

This is made the same as Brandy Sangaree, substituting Holland gin instead of brandy.

❖❖❖

153. ALE SANGAREE

(Use large bar-glass)

Take 1 teaspoonful of fine white sugar dissolved
     in a wine glassful of water

Fill up the glass with ale, stir, and grate a little nutmeg on top.

❖❖❖

154. GIN PUNCH

(Use large bar-glass)

Take 1 tablespoonful of raspberry syrup

1 tablespoonful of powdered white sugar, dissolved
     in a little Seltzer water

1½ wine-glasses of Holland gin

Juice of half a small lemon

1 slice of orange (cut in quarters)

1 piece of pineapple

1 or 2 dashes of Maraschino

Fill the tumbler with shaved ice, shake well, and dress the top with sliced lime and berries in season.

155. HOT IRISH WHISKEY PUNCH

(Use medium bar-glass)

Take 1 wine-glass Kinahan's or Jamieson's Irish
  whiskey

2 wine-glasses of boiling water

2 lumps of loaf-sugar

Dissolve the sugar well with one wine-glass of the water,
then pour in the whiskey, add the balance of the water,
and put in a small piece of lemon rind, or a thin slice
of lemon. Before using the glass, rinse it in hot water.

⟡⟡⟡

156. HOT SCOTCH WHISKEY PUNCH

(Use medium bar-glass)

Take 1 wine-glass of Glenlivet or Islay whiskey

2 wine-glasses of boiling water

Sugar to taste (about 2 lumps of loaf sugar)

Dissolve the sugar with one wine-glass of the water,
then pour in the whiskey, add the balance of the water,
and put in a small piece of lemon rind or a thin slice
of lemon. Before using the glass rinse it in hot water.

⟡⟡⟡

157. COLD WHISKEY PUNCH

(Use large bar-glass)

Take 1 tablespoonful of powdered white sugar dissolved in a little water

Juice of half a small lemon

1½ wine-glasses of Irish or Scotch whiskey

Fill the glass with shaved ice, shake well, and dress the top with two thin slices of lemon, and berries in season. Serve with a straw.

<><><>

158. ARRACK PUNCH

(Use medium bar-glass)

Take 1 tablespoonful of powdered white sugar dissolved in a little water

Juice of half a small lemon

1 pony-glass of Batavia arrack

1 wine-glass of Jamaica rum

1 piece of pineapple

Fill the glass with shaved ice, shake well, and dress the top with berries in season. Serve with a straw.

<><><>

159. MILK PUNCH

(Use large bar-glass)

Take 1 teaspoonful of fine white sugar

1 wine-glass of brandy

½ wine-glass of Santa Cruz rum

Small lump of ice

Fill with milk, shake the ingredients well together, strain into a large glass, and grate a little nutmeg on top.

<><><>

160. HOT MILK PUNCH

(Use large bar-glass)

This punch is made the same as the above, with the exception that hot milk is used, and no ice.

161. MANHATTAN MILK PUNCH

(Use large bar-glass)

Same as the foregoing cold milk punch, with the addition of five drops of Aromatic tincture.

◇━◇

162. EGG MILK PUNCH

(Use large bar-glass)

Take 1 teaspoonful of fine white sugar

1 wine-glass of brandy

½ wine-glass of Santa Cruz rum

1 egg

Small lump of ice

Fill the glass with pure fresh milk, shake the ingredients well together and strain into a large glass.

◇━◇

163. CLARET PUNCH

(Use large bar-glass)

Take 1 teaspoonful of fine sugar

1 slice of lemon

1 slice of orange (cut in quarters)

Fill the tumbler two-thirds full of shaved ice, then pour in the claret until the glass is full, shake well, and ornament with berries in season. Serve with a straw.

164. SAUTERNE PUNCH

(Use large bar-glass)
Take 1 teaspoonful of fine white sugar
1 slice of lemon
1 slice of orange
1 piece of pineapple
Fill the tumbler two-thirds full with shaved ice, then pour in the Sauterne until the glass is full, shake well, and dress with berries in season.

<><><>

165. VANILLA PUNCH

(Use large bar-glass)
Take 1 tablespoonful of sugar
1 wine-glass of brandy
The juice of quarter of a lemon
Fill the tumbler with shaved ice, shake well, ornament with one or two slices of lemon, and flavor with a few drops of vanilla extract. This is a delicious drink, and should be imbibed through a glass tube or straw.

<><><>

166. SHERRY PUNCH

(Use small bar-glass)
Take 2 wine-glasses of sherry
1 teaspoonful of sugar
1 slice of orange
1 slice of lemon
Fill tumbler with shaved ice, shake well, and ornament with berries in season. Serve with a straw.

167. ROMAN PUNCH

(Use small bar-glass)

Take 1 tablespoonful of powdered white sugar, dissolved in a little water

1 tablespoonful of raspberry syrup

1 teaspoonful of Curaçoa

1 wine-glass of Jamaica rum

½ wine-glass of brandy

The juice of half a lemon

Fill with shaved ice, shake well, dash with Port wine,
and ornament with fruits in season. Serve with a straw.

◇◇◇

168. CHAMPAGNE PUNCH

(One quart of punch)

Take 1 quart bottle of Champagne wine

3 tablespoonfuls of sugar

1 orange sliced

The juice of a lemon

2 slices of pineapple (cut in small pieces)

1 wine-glass of raspberry or strawberry syrup

Ornament with fruits in season, and serve in Champagne goblets. This can be made in any quantity by
observing the proportions of the ingredients as given
above. Four bottles of wine make a gallon, and a gallon
is generally sufficient for fifteen persons in a mixed party.

169. MISSISSIPPI PUNCH

(Use large bar-glass)
Take 1 wine-glass of brandy
½ wine-glass of Jamaica rum
½ wine-glass of Bourbon whiskey
1 tablespoonful of powdered white sugar, dissolved
in a little water
The juice of half a small lemon
Fill the glass with shaved ice, shake well, and ornament
with fruit in season. Serve with a straw.

⬦⬦⬦

170. IMPERIAL PUNCH

(For a party of twenty)
Take 1 gallon of water
3 quarts of brandy
1 pint of Jamaica rum
1½ pounds of white sugar
Juice of 6 lemons
3 oranges sliced
1 pineapple, pared and cut up
1 gill of Curaçoa
2 gills of raspberry syrup
Ice, and add berries in season
Mix the materials well together in a large bowl, and
you have a splendid punch. If not sweet enough, add
more sugar.

171. HOT BRANDY AND RUM PUNCH

(For a party of fifteen)
Take 1 quart of Jamaica rum
1 quart of Cognac brandy
1 pound of white loaf-sugar
4 lemons
3 quarts of boiling water
1 teaspoonful of nutmeg

Rub the sugar over the lemons until it has absorbed all the yellow part of the skins, then put the sugar into a punch-bowl; add the ingredients well together, pour over them the boiling water, stir well together; add the rum, brandy and nutmeg; mix thoroughly, and the punch will be ready to serve.

<><><>

172. ALE PUNCH

Take 1 quart of mild ale
1 glass of white wine
1 glass of brandy
1 glass of Capillaire
1 lemon

Mix the ale, wine, brandy and Capillaire together with the juice of the lemon, and a portion of the peel pared very thin. Grate nutmeg on the top and add a bit of toasted bread.

173. CIDER PUNCH

Take ½ pint of Sherry
1 glass of brandy
1 bottle of cider
½ pound of sugar
1 lemon

Pare the peel of half the lemon very thin; pour the Sherry upon it; add the sugar, the juice of the lemon, and the cider, with a little grated nutmeg. Mix well and place it on ice. When cold, add the brandy and a few pieces of cucumber rind.

❖❖❖

174. HOT ENGLISH RUM FLIP

(One quart)
Take 1 quart of ale
1 gill of old rum
4 raw fresh eggs
4 ounces of moist sugar
1 teaspoonful of grated nutmeg (of ginger)

Heat the ale in a saucepan; beat up the eggs and sugar, add the nutmeg and rum, and put it all in a pitcher. When the ale is near to a boil, put it in another pitcher, pour it very gradually in the pitcher containing the eggs, etc., stirring all the while very briskly to prevent the eggs from curdling, then pour the contents of the two pitchers from one to the other until the mixture is as smooth as cream.

175. HOT ENGLISH ALE FLIP

(One quart)

This is prepared in the same manner as Rum Flip, omitting the rum, and the whites of two of the eggs.

◇◇◇

176. SLEEPER

Take 1 gill of old rum
1 ounce of sugar
2 fresh raw eggs
½ pint of water
6 cloves
6 coriander seeds
1 lemon

Boil the cloves and coriander, with a bit of cinnamon in the water; mix together the rum, sugar, the yolks of the eggs and the juice of half the lemon; whisk them all together, and strain into a tumbler.

◇◇◇

177. WHITE TIGER'S MILK

(From a recipe in the possession of Dr. Thomas
    Dunn English)

Take ½ gill of apple jack
½ gill of peach brandy
½ teaspoonful of aromatic tincture
Sweeten with white sugar to taste
The white of an egg beaten to a stiff foam
1 quart of pure fresh milk

Pour in the milk to the mixed liquors, gradually, stirring all the while till all is well mixed, then sprinkle with nutmeg. The above recipe is sufficient to make a full quart of "White Tiger's Milk"; if more is wanted, you can increase the above proportions. If you want to prepare this beverage for a party of twenty, use one gallon of milk to one pint of apple jack, etc.

<><><>

178. BRANDY STRAIGHT

(Use small bar-glass)

In serving this drink you simply put a piece of ice in a tumbler, and hand it to your customer, with the bottle of brandy, and a separate glass of ice water.

Whiskey Straight and Gin Straight are served in the same manner.

<><><>

179. PONY BRANDY

(Use small bar-glass)

Take 1 pony-glass of brandy (best)

Pour it into the glass, and serve with some icewater in a separate glass

Some bartenders have a fancy way of serving this drink

It is done thusly:

Fill to the brim a pony-glass of brandy, cover it with the bar-glass, then press both glasses tightly together and turn them over quickly, so that the pony-glass will remain upside down in the bar-glass, without a drop of the brandy escaping.

180. BRANDY AND SODA

(Use large soda-water glass)
Take 1 wine-glass of brandy
2 or 3 small lumps of ice
Fill up the glass with a bottle of plain soda-water. This is sometimes called STONE WALL.

⬦⬦⬦

181. BRANDY AND GINGER ALE

(Use large soda-water glass)
Take 1 wine-glass of brandy
2 or 3 small lumps of ice
Fill up the glass with Irish ginger ale

⬦⬦⬦

182. SPLIT SODA AND BRANDY

(Use medium bar-glass)
Take 1 pony-glass of brandy
1 small lump of ice
Add one-half of a bottle of plain soda-water.

⬦⬦⬦

183. RHINE WINE AND SELTZER WATER

(Use large bar-glass)
Pour in Rhine wine until the glass is half full
Add two small lumps of ice
Fill the glass with Seltzer water

184. SHANDY GAFF

(Use large bar-glass, or mug)

Fill the glass half full of Ale, and the remaining
half with Irish ginger ale

In England, where this drink had its origin, it is
made with Bass' Ale, and Ginger ale, half and
half

◇-◇-◇

185. HALF AND HALF

(Use metal or stone bar-mug)

Mix half old and half new ale together

This is the American method.

◇-◇-◇

186. "ARF AND ARF"

(Use metal or stone bar-mug)

Mix porter or Stout, with Ale in equal quantities,
or in proportions to suit the taste

This is the English method, and usually, "Draw it
mild, Mary, the ale first."

◇-◇-◇

187. ABSINTHE AND WATER

(Use large bar-glass)

Take 1 pony-glass of Absinthe

Fill an absinthe glass (which is a glass made purposely
with a hole in the bottom), with shaved ice and water.
Raise this glass about one foot above the tumbler containing the absinthe, and let sufficient water drip into it.

188. FRENCH METHOD OF SERVING ABSINTHE

(Use Champagne glass standing in a bowl)
Take 1 pony-glass of Absinthe
Let the water drip, as directed in the preceding recipe,
until the glass is full, and a very little runs over into
the bowl.

<><><>

189. ROCK AND RYE

(Use small bar-glass)
Take 1 tablespoonful of rock-candy syrup
1 wine-glass of rye whiskey
Stir them together thoroughly, and serve.
This is often prescribed for a cold.

<><><>

190. STONE FENCE

(Use large bar-glass)
Take 1 wine-glass of Bourbon or rye whiskey
2 or 3 small lumps of ice
Fill up the glass with sweet cider.

<><><>

191. BRANDY COCKTAIL FOR BOTTLING

Take 5 gallons of spirits (70 per cent)
2 gallons of water
1 quart of gum syrup
¼ pint essence of Cognac
1 ounce of tincture of cloves
1 ounce of tincture of gentian

2 ounces of tincture of orange peel

¼ ounce of tincture of cardamom

½ ounce of tincture of licorice root

Mix the essence and tinctures with a portion of the spirits; add the remainder of the ingredients, and color with a sufficient quantity of Solferino and caramel (in equal parts) to give the desired color.

<><><>

192. GIN COCKTAIL FOR BOTTLING

Take 5 gallons of gin

2 gallons of water

1 quart of gum syrup

2 ounces of tincture of orange peel

7 ounces of tincture of gentian

½ ounce of tincture of cardamom

½ ounce of tincture of lemon peel

Mix them together, and give the desired color with Solferino and caramel, in equal proportions.

<><><>

193. BOURBON COCKTAIL FOR BOTTLING

Take 5 gallons of Bourbon

2 gallons of water

1 quart of gum syrup

2 ounces of tincture of orange peel

1 ounce of tincture of lemon peel

1 ounce of tincture of gentian

½ ounce of tincture of cardamom

Mix these ingredients thoroughly, and color with Solferino and caramel, in equal proportions.

Eleven Famous Cocktails

of the

Most Exclusive Club

of

New York

As Served Before the War

When Mixing Drinks Was an Art

1. BRONX

One-third Italian and French Vermouth
Two-thirds Dry Gin
Slice of Orange
} *Frappé*

<><><>

2. ASTOR

One-half of Lime
Large Slice of Orange
One-third Caloric Punch
One-third Dry Gin
} *Frappé*

<><><>

3. BACARDI

One-half of Lime
One-quarter Grenadine
Three-quarters Bacardi Rum
} *Frappé*

<><><>

4. CLOVER

One-half of Lime
White of One Egg
One-quarter Grenadine
One-half Dry Gin
} *Frappé*

<><><>

5. DRY MARTINI

One-third French Vermouth
Two-thirds Dry Gin
} *Frappé*

6. PERFECT

One-third Italian and French Vermouth ⎱
Two-thirds Dry Gin ⎰ *Frappé*

<><><>

7. COOPERSTOWN

One-third Italian and French Vermouth ⎫
Two-thirds Dry Gin ⎪
Slice of Orange ⎬ *Frappé*
Sprig of fresh mint ⎭

<><><>

8. CHRIS

One-third Italian Vermouth ⎱
Two-thirds Plymouth Gin ⎰ *Frappé*

<><><>

9. MARTINI

One-third Italian Vermouth ⎱
Two-thirds Dry Gin ⎰ *Frappé*

<><><>

10. LIBERTY

One-half Italian Vermouth ⎫
One-half Plymouth Gin ⎬ *Frappé*
Oil of Orange Peel ⎭

<><><>

11. MANHATTAN

Two-thirds Rye Whiskey ⎱
One-third Italian Vermouth ⎰ *Stirred*

HOME-MADE WINE

WINES

GENERAL DIRECTIONS FOR WINE MAKING

The best method of making these wines is to boil the ingredients, and ferment with yeast. Boiling makes the wine more soft and mellow. Some, however, mix the juice, or juice and fruit, with sugar and water unboiled, and leave the ingredients to ferment spontaneously. Your fruit should always be prime, and gathered dry, and picked clean from stalks, etc. The lees of wine are valuable for distillation, or making vinegar. When wine is put in the cask the fermentation will be renewed. Clear away the yeast as it rises, and fill up with wine, for which purposes a small quantity should be reserved. If brandy is to be added, it must be when the fermentation has nearly subsided, that is, when no more yeast is thrown up at the bung-hole, and when the hissing noise is not very perceptible; thus mix a quart of brandy with a pound of honey, pour into the cask, and paste stiff brown paper over the bung-hole. Allow no hole for a vent peg, lest it should once be forgotten, and the whole cask of wine be spoiled. If the wine wants vent it will be sure to burst the paper; if not the paper will sufficiently exclude the air. Once a week or so it may be looked to; if the paper is burst, renew it, and continue to do so until it remains clear and dry.

A great difference of opinion prevails as to racking the wine, or suffering it to remain on the lees. Those who adopt the former plan do it at the end of six months; draw off the wine perfectly clear, and put it into a fresh cask, in which it is to remain six months, and then be bottled. If this plan is adopted, it may be better, instead of putting the brandy and honey in the first cask, to put it in that in which the wine is to be racked; but on the whole, it is, perhaps, preferable to leave the wine a year in the first cask, and then bottle it at once.

All British wines improve in the cask more than in the bottle. Have very nice clear and dry bottles; do not fill them too high. Good soft corks, made supple by soaking in a little of the wine; press them in, but do not knock. Keep the bottles lying in sawdust. This plan will apply equally well to raspberries, cherries, mulberries, and all kinds of ripe summer fruits.

◇◇◇

194. COLORING FOR WINES

One pound of white sugar. Put into an iron kettle, let boil, and burn to a red black, and thick; remove from the fire, and add a little hot water, to keep it from hardening as it cools; then bottle for use.

195. FINING OR CLEARING

For fining or clearing the wine use one quarter pound of isinglass, dissolved in a portion of the wine, to a barrel. This must be put in after the fermentation is over, and should be added gently at the bung-hole, and managed so as to spread as much as possible over the upper surface of the liquid; the intention being that the isinglass should unite with impurities and carry them with it to the bottom.

❖❖❖

196. TO FLAVOR WINE

When the vinous fermentation is about half over, the flavoring ingredients are to be put into the vat and well stirred into the contents. If almonds form a component part, they are first to be beaten to a paste and mixed with a pint or two of the must. Nutmegs, cinnamon, ginger, seeds, etc., should, before they are put into the vat, be reduced to powder, and mixed with some of the must.

❖❖❖

197. TO MELLOW WINE

Wine, either in bottle or wood, will mellow much quicker when only covered with pieces of bladder well secured, than with corks or bungs. The bladder allows the watery particles to escape, but is impervious to alcohol.

198. TO REMOVE THE TASTE OF THE CASK FROM WINE

Finest oil of olives, one pound. Put it into the hogshead, bung close, and roll it about, or otherwise well agitate it, for three or four hours, then gib, and allow it to settle. The olive oil will gradually rise to the top and carry the ill flavor with it.

◇◇◇

199. TO REMOVE ROPINESS FROM WINE

Add a little catechu or a small quantity of the bruised berries of the mountain ash.

◇◇◇

200. TO RESTORE WINE WHEN SOUR OR SHARP

1. Fill a bag with leek-seed, or with leaves or twisters of vine, and put either of them to infuse in the cask. 2. Put a small quantity of powdered charcoal in the wine, shake it, and after it has remained still for forty-eight hours, decant steadily.

◇◇◇

201. TO MAKE APPLE WINE

To every gallon of apple juice, immediately as it comes from the press, add two pounds of common loaf sugar; boil it as long as any scum rises, then strain it through a sieve, and let it cool. Add some good yeast, and stir it well. Let it work in the tub for two or three weeks, or till the head begins to flatten; then skim off the head, drain it clear off and tun it. When made a year, rack it off and fine it with isinglass; then add one-half pint of the best rectified spirit of wine or a pint of French brandy to every eight gallons.

◇–◇–◇

202. APRICOT WINE

Take three pounds of sugar, and three quarts of water; let them boil together and skim it well. Then put in six pounds of apricots, pared and stoned, and let them boil until they are tender; then take them up and when the liquor is cold bottle it up. You may if you please, after you have taken out the apricots, let the liquor have one boil with a sprig of flowered clary in it; the apricots make marmalade, and are very good for preserves.

◇–◇–◇

203. BLACKBERRY WINE

Bruise the berries well with the hands. To one gallon of fruit, add one-half gallon of water, and let stand overnight. Strain and measure, and to each gallon of juice add two and one-half pounds of sugar. Put in cask and let ferment. Tack thin muslin over top, and when fermentation stops, pour into jugs or kegs. Wine keeps best in kegs.

204. AMERICAN CHAMPAGNE

7 quarts good cider (crab-apple cider is the best), 1 pint best fourth-proof brandy, 1 quart genuine champagne wine, 1 quart milk, ½ ounce of bitartrate of potassa. Mix and let stand a short time; bottle while fermenting.

◇–◇–◇

205. BRITISH CHAMPAGNE

To every 5 pounds of rhubarb, when sliced and bruised, put 1 gallon of cold spring water. Let it stand 3 days, stirring 2 or 3 times every day; then press and strain it through a sieve, and to every gallon of liquor, put three and one-half pounds of loaf sugar. Stir it well, and when melted, barrel it. When it has done working, bung it up close, first suspending a muslin bag with isinglass from the bung into the barrel. To 8 gallons of liquor, put 2 ounces of isinglass. In 6 months bottle it and wire the bottles; let them stand up for the first month, then lay four or five down lengthways for a week, and if none burst, all may be laid down. Should a large quantity be made, it must remain longer in the cask. It may be colored pink by putting in a quart of raspberry juice. It will keep for many years.

◇–◇–◇

206. BURGUNDY CHAMPAGNE

14 pounds loaf sugar, 12 pounds brown sugar (pale), 10 gallons warm water, 1 ounce white tartar. Mix, and

at a proper temperature add 1 pint yeast. Afterwards, add 1 gallon sweet cider, 2 or 3 bitter almonds (bruised), 1 quart pale spirit, ⅛ ounce orris powder.

◇◇◇

207. CHAMPAGNE CIDER

One hogshead good pale vinous cider, 3 gallons proof spirit (pale), 14 pounds honey or sugar. Mix, and let them remain together in a temperate situation for one month; then add 1 quart orange-flower water, and fine it down with ½ gallon skimmed milk. This will be very pale; and a similar article, when bottled in champagne bottles, silvered and labelled, has been often sold to the ignorant for champagne. It opens very brisk, if managed properly.

◇◇◇

208. SHAM CHAMPAGNE

1 lemon sliced, 1 tablespoon tartaric acid, 1 ounce of race-ginger, one and one-half pounds sugar, 2½ gallons of boiling water, poured on the above. When blood warm, add 1 gill of distillery yeast, or 2 gills of home-brewed. Let it stand in the sun through the day. When cold, in the evening, bottle, cork and wire it. In 2 days it is ready for use.

◇◇◇

209. SHERRY BOUNCE

1 gallon of good whiskey, 1½ pints of wild black cherries bruised so as to break the stones, 2 ounces of

common almonds shelled, 2 ounces of white sugar, ½ teaspoonful cinnamon, ¼ teaspoonful cinnamon, ¼ teaspoonful cloves, ¼ teaspoonful nutmeg, all bruised. Let stand 12 to 13 days, and draw off. This, with the addition of ½ gallon of brandy, makes very nice cherry bounce.

◇—◇—◇

210. TO MAKE CHERRY WINE

Pull off the stalks of the cherries, and mash them without breaking the stones; then press them hard through a hair bag, and to every gallon of liquor, put 2 pounds of sugar. The vessel must be full, and let it work as long as it makes a noise in the vessel; then stop it up close for a month or more, and when it is fine, draw it into dry bottles, and put a lump of sugar into every bottle. If it makes them fly, open them all for a moment, and then stop them up again. It will be fit to drink in a quarter of a year.

◇—◇—◇

211. BOILING CIDER

To prepare cider for boiling, the first process is to filter it immediately on coming from the press. This is easiest done by placing some sticks crosswise in the bottom of a barrel,—a flour barrel with a single head is the best,—wherein an inch hole has been bored, and covering these sticks with say four inches of clean rye or wheat straw, and then filling the barrel to within a foot of the top with clean sand or coal dust,—sand is the best. Pour the cider as it comes from the press into the top of this barrel, drawing it off as soon as it comes out at the bottom into air-tight casks, and let it stand in the cellar until March. Then draw it out with as little exposure to the air as possible, put it into bottles that can be tightly and securely corked, and in two months it will be fit for use.

<hr/>

212. TO CLEAR CIDER

To clear and improve cider generally take 2 quarts of ground horseradish and 1 pound of thick gray filtering paper to the barrel, and either shake or stir until the paper has separated into small shreds, and let it stand for 24 hours, when the cider may be drawn off by means of a siphon or a stop cock. Instead of paper, a preparation of wool may be taken, which is to be had in the market, and which is preferable to paper, as it has simply to be washed with water, when it may be used again.

<hr/>

213. CIDER CHAMPAGNE

5 gallons good cider, 1 quart spirit, 1¼ pounds of honey or sugar. Mix and let them rest for a fortnight, then fine with 1 gill of skimmed milk. This, put up in champagne bottles, silvered, and labelled, has often been sold for champagne. It opens very sparkling.

214. CIDER WINE

Let the new cider from sour apples (ripe, sound fruit preferred) ferment from one to three weeks, as the weather is warm or cool. When it has attained to a lively fermentation, add to each gallon, according to acidity, from ½ pound to 2 pounds of white crushed sugar, and let the whole ferment until it possesses precisely the taste which it is desired should be permanent. In this condition pour out one quart of the cider, and add for each gallon of cider ¼ ounce of sulphite of lime, not sulphate. Stir the powder and cider until intimately mixed, and return the emulsion to the fermenting liquid. Agitate briskly and thoroughly for a few moments, and then let the cider settle. Fermentation will cease at once. When, after a few days, the cider has become clear, draw off carefully, to avoid the sediment, and bottle. If loosely corked, which is better, it will become a sparkling cider wine, and may be kept indefinitely long.

◇◇◇

215. TO MAKE FINE CLARY WINE

To 5 gallons of water put 12½ pounds of sugar, and the whites of 6 eggs well beaten. Set it over the fire, and let it boil gently near an hour; skim it clean and put it in a tub, and when it is near cold, then put into the vessel you keep it in about ½ a strike of clary in the blossom, stripped from the stalks, flowers and little leaves together, and 1 pint of new ale-yeast. Then put in the liquor, and stir it 2 or 3 times a day for 3 days; when it has done working, stop it up, and bottle it at 3 or 4 months old, if it is clear.

◇-◇-◇

216. CURRANT WINE

Take 4 gallons of currants, not too ripe, and strip them into an earthen stein that has a cover to it. Then take 2½ gallons of water and 5½ pounds of double refined sugar; boil the sugar and water together, skim it, and pour it boiling hot on the currants, letting it stand 48 hours; then strain it through a flannel bag into the stein again, let it stand a fortnight to settle, and bottle it out.

◇-◇-◇

217. DAISY WINE

1 quart of daisy heads, 1 quart of cold water. Let stand 48 hours. Strain and add ¾ pound of sugar to each quart of liquid. Let stand about 2 weeks, till it stops fermenting. Strain again and bottle. It improves with keeping.

◇-◇-◇

218. DANDELION WINE

4 quarts of dandelions. Cover with 4 quarts of boiling water; let stand 3 days. Add peel of three oranges and one lemon. Boil 15 minutes; drain and add juice of oranges and lemon to 4 pounds of sugar and 1 cup of yeast. Keep in warm room and strain; let it stand for 3 weeks. It is then ready to bottle and serve.

219. ELDER FLOWER WINE

Take the flowers of elder, and be careful that you don't let any stalks in; to every quart of flowers put 1 gallon of water, and 3 pounds of loaf sugar. Boil the water and sugar a quarter of an hour, then pour it on the flowers and let it work 3 days; then strain the wine through a hair sieve, and put it into a cask. To every 10 gallons of wine add 1 ounce of isinglass dissolved in cider, and 6 whole eggs. Close it up and let it stand 6 months, and then bottle it.

220. ELDERBERRY WINE

9 quarts of elderberry juice, 9 quarts water, 11½ pounds white sugar, 2 ounces red tartar. These are put into a cask, a little yeast added, and the whole is fermented. When undergoing fermentation, 1 ounce ginger root, 1 ounce allspice, ¼ ounce cloves are put into a bag of clean cotton cloth, and suspended in the cask. They will give a pleasant flavor to the wine, which will become clear in about 2 months, and may be drawn off and bottled. Add some brandy to this wine, but if the fermentation is properly conducted, this is not necessary.

221. ENGLISH FIG WINE

Take the large blue figs when pretty ripe, and steep them in white wine, having made some slits in them, that they may swell and gather in the substance of the wine.

Then slice some other figs and let them simmer over a fire in water until they are reduced to a kind of pulp. Then strain out the water, pressing the pulp hard and pour it as hot as possible on the figs that are imbrued in the wine. Let the quantities be nearly equal, but the water somewhat more than the wine and figs. Let them stand 24 hours, mash them well together, and draw off what will run without squeezing. Then press the rest, and if not sweet enough add a sufficient quantity of sugar to make it so. Let it ferment, and add to it a little honey and sugar candy, then fine it with white of eggs, and a little isinglass, and draw it off for use.

<><><>

222. TO MAKE FRONTIGNAC WINE

Take 3 gallons of water, 6 pounds of white sugar, and 3 pounds of raisins of the sun cut small; boil these together an hour. Then take of the flowers of elder, when they are falling, and will shake off, the quantity of half a peck; put them in the liquor when it is almost cold. The next day put in 3 spoonfuls of syrup of lemons and 2 spoonfuls of ale-yeast, and 2 days after put it in a vessel that is fit for it, and when it has stood 2 months, bottle it off.

<><><>

223. TO MAKE GOOSEBERRY WINE

Boil 4 gallons of water, and ½ pound of sugar an hour, skim it well, and let it stand till it is cold. Then to every quart of that water, allow 1½ pounds of gooseberries, first beaten or bruised very well, let it stand 24 hours. Then strain it out, and to every gallon of this liquor put 3 pounds of sugar; let it stand in the vat 12 hours. Then take the thick scum off, and put the clear into a vessel fit for it, and let it stand a month; then draw it off, and rinse the vessel with some of the liquor. Put it in again, and let it stand four months, and bottle it.

❖❖❖

224. RED AND WHITE GOOSEBERRY WINE

Take one and one-half gallons cold soft water, 3 quarts red gooseberries, 2 quarts white gooseberries. Ferment. Now mix 2½ pounds raw sugar, ¾ pound honey, ½ ounce tartar in fine powder. Afterwards put in 1 ounce bitter almonds, a small handful sweet briar, 2 quarts brandy or less.

❖❖❖

225. WHITE GOOSEBERRY OR CHAMPAGNE WINE

Take 4½ gallons cold soft water and 15 quarts of white gooseberries. Ferment. Now mix 6 pounds refined sugar, 4 pounds honey, 1 ounce white tartar in fine powder. Put in one ounce dry orange and lemon peel, or 2 ounces fresh, and add ½ gallon white brandy. This will make 9 gallons.

❖❖❖

226. GRAPE WINE

2 quarts of grape juice, 2 quarts of water, 4 pounds of sugar. Extract the juice of the grape in any simple way;

if only a few quarts are desired, we do it with a strainer and a pair of squeezers; if a large quantity is desired, put the grapes into a cheese-press made particularly clean, putting on sufficient weight to extract the juice of a full hoop of grapes, being careful that none but perfect grapes are used, perfectly ripe and free from blemish. After the first pressing, put a little water with the pulp and press a second time, using the juice of the second pressing with the water to be mixed with the clear grape juice. If only a few quarts are made, place the wine as soon as mixed into bottles, filling them even full, and allow to stand in a warm place until it ferments, which will take about 36 hours usually; then remove all the scum, cool, and put into a dark, cool place. If a few gallons are desired, place in a keg, but the keg must be even full, and after fermentation has taken place and the scum removed, draw off and bottle, and cork tight.

<><><>

227. HOT BEER

Turn 5 quarts of water on 6 ounces of hops; boil three hours. Strain off the liquor; turn on 4 quarts more of water, and 12 spoonfuls of ginger, and boil the hops 3 hours longer. Strain and mix it with the other liquor, and stir in 2 quarts of molasses. Brown, very dry, ½ pound of bread, and put in,—rusked bread is best. Pound it fine, and brown it in a pot, like coffee. After cooling to be about lukewarm, add 1 pint of new yeast that is free from salt. Keep the beer covered, in a temperate situation, till fermentation has ceased, which is known by the settling of the froth; then turn it into a keg or bottles, and keep it in a cool place.

◇◇◇

228. JUNIPER-BERRY WINE

Take 4½ gallons of cold soft water, 7 pounds Malaga or Smyrna raisins, 2¼ quarts juniper-berries, ½ ounce red tartar, ½ handful wormwood, ½ handful sweet marjoram, 1 pint whiskey or more. Ferment for 10 or 12 days.

◇◇◇

229. LEMON WINE

4 pounds sugar, 1 pound raisins (bruised), 2 gallons water. Boil, then add 1 gallon cider. Ferment, and add 1 quart of spirits, ¾ ounce white tartar, a few drops essence of lemon. Observe to shake the essence, with a little of the spirit, until it becomes milky, before adding it to the wine.

◇◇◇

230. MADEIRA WINE

To 5 gallons prepared cider, add ½ ounce tartaric acid, ½ pint spirits, ½ pound loaf sugar. Let it stand 10 days, draw it off carefully, fine it down, and again rack it into another cask.

231. MALT WINE, OR ENGLISH SHERRY

Take 12 pounds of good moist sugar, 2 gallons of water. Boil them together 2 hours, skimming carefully. When the scum is all removed, and the liquor looks clear, add ½ ounce of hops, which should boil ¼ hour or 20 minutes. When the liquor is quite cold, add to it 5 quarts of strong beer in the height of working; cover up and let it work 48 hours; then skim and tun. If none remains, for filling up, use new beer for that purpose. This method may be adopted with all boiled wines, and will be found to improve their strength and promote their keeping. In a fortnight or 3 weeks, when the head begins to sink, add 2½ pounds raisins (free from stalks), 1 ounce of sugar candy, 1 ounce of bitter almonds, ½ cup of the best brandy; brown paper, as in former articles. It may be bottled in one year; but if left 3 years in the wood, and then bottled, it will be found equal in strength and flavor to foreign wine.

❖❖❖

232. TO MAKE ORANGE WINE

Put 12 pounds of fine sugar and the whites of 8 eggs well beaten into 6 gallons of spring water; let it boil an hour, skimming it all the time. Take it off and when it is pretty cool, put in the juice and rind of fifty Seville oranges, and 6 spoonfuls of good ale yeast, and let it stand 2 days. Then put it into your vessel, with 2 quarts of Rhenish wine, and the juice of 12 lemons. You must let the juice of lemons and wine and 2 pounds of double refined sugar stand close covered 10 or 12 hours before you put it in the vessel to your orange wine, and skim off the seeds before you put it in. The lemon peels must be put in with the oranges; half the rinds must be put into the vessel. It must stand 10 or 12 days before it is fit to bottle.

◇–◇–◇

233. TO MAKE PALERMO WINE

Take to every quart of water 1 pound of Malaga raisins, rub and cut the raisins small, and put them to the water, and let them stand 10 days, stirring once or twice a day. You may boil the water an hour before you put it to the raisins, and let it stand to cool. At ten days' end strain out your liquor, and put a little yeast to it; and at three days' end put it in the vessel, with one sprig of dried wormwood. Let it be close stopped, and at 3 months' end bottle it off.

◇–◇–◇

234. TO MAKE PEACH WINE

Take 3 gallons cold soft water, 4¼ pounds refined sugar, 1 pound honey, ⅓ ounce white tartar in fine powder, 10 or 14 peaches. Ferment; then add six quarts of brandy. The first division is to be put into a vat, and the day after, before the peaches are put in, take the stones from them, break these and the kernels, then put them and the pulp into a vat and proceed with the general process.

235. PLUM WINE

Take 5 pounds of Malaga raisins, pick, rub and shred them, and put them into a tub; then take one gallon of water, boil it an hour, and let it stand till it is blood-warm; then put it to your raisins. Let it stand 9 or 10 days, stirring it once or twice a day; strain out your liquor, and mix it with one pint of damson juice. Put it in a vessel, and when it has done working stop it close; at 4 or 5 months bottle it.

❖❖❖

236. PORTER

8 quarters pale malt, 6 quarters amber malt, 2 quarters brown malt. Mash it twice, with 55 and 48 barrels of water, then boil with one hundredweight of Kent hops, and set with 10 gallons yeast, 7 pounds salt, 2 pounds flour. 20 barrels of good table beer may be had from the grains. If deficient in color, add burnt malt.

❖❖❖

237. PORTER, FOR BOTTLING

5 quarters pale malt, 3 quarters amber malt, 2 quarters brown malt, burnt malt to color if required. Mash with 24, 14 and 11 barrels of water, then boil with one hundredweight Kent hops, and set with seven gallons yeast, 3 pounds salt. Mash the grains for table beer.

238. PORT WINE

To 10 gallons prepared cider, add 1½ gallons good Port wine, 2½ quarts wild grapes (clusters), 2 ounces bruised rhatany root, ¾ ounce tincture of kino, ¾ pound loaf sugar, ½ gallon spirits. Let this stand 10 days; color if too light, with tincture of rhatany, then rack it off and fine it. This should be repeated until the color is perfect and the liquid clear.

◇-◇-◇

239. RAISIN WINE

5 pounds of raisins, 4 gallons of water. Put them into a cask. Mash for a fortnight, frequently stirring, and leave the lung loose until the active fermentation ceases; then add 1½ pints of brandy. Well mix, and let it stand till fine. The quantity of raisins and brandy may be altered to suit.

◇-◇-◇

240. RAISIN WINE WITH SUGAR

To every gallon of soft water 4 pounds of fresh raisins; put them in a large tub; stir frequently, and keep it covered with a sack or blanket. In about a fortnight the fermentation will begin to subside; this may be known by the raisins remaining still. Then press the fruit and strain the liquor. Have ready a wine cask, perfectly dry and warm, allowing for each gallon one or one and one-half pounds of Lisbon sugar; put this into a cask with the strained liquor. When half full, stir well the sugar and liquor, and put in 1.2 pint of thick yeast; then fill up with the liquor, and continue to do so while the fermentation lasts, which will be a month or more.

◇◇◇

241. TO MAKE RASPBERRY WINE

Take your quantity of raspberries and bruise them, put them in an open pot 24 hours; then squeeze out the juice, and to every gallon of the juice put 3 pounds of fine sugar, 2 quarts of canary. Put it into a stein or vessel, and when it has done working stop it close; when it is fine, bottle it. It must stand 2 months before you drink it.

◇◇◇

242. RASPBERRY WINE

Pound your fruit and strain it through a cloth; then boil as much water as juice of raspberries, and when it is cold put it to your squeezings. Let it stand together 5 hours, then strain it and mix it with the juice, adding to every gallon of this liquor 2½ pounds of fine sugar. Let it stand in an earthen vessel close covered a week, then put it in a vessel fit for it, and let it stand a month or till it is fine; bottle it off.

243. RHUBARB WINE

To each gallon of juice add 1 gallon of soft water, in which 7 pounds of brown sugar have been dissolved. Fill a keg or a barrel with this proportion, leaving the bung out, and keep it filled with sweetened water as it works over until clear; then bung down or bottle as you desire. These stalks will furnish about ¾ their weight in juice, or from 1600 to 2000 gallons of wine to each acre of well cultivated plants. Fill the barrels and let them stand until spring, and bottle, as any wine will be better in glass or stone.

244. SHERRY WINE

To 5 gallons prepared cider add 1 quart spirits, ¾ of a pound of raisins, ¾ good sherry, and a few drops oil of bitter almonds (dissolved in alcohol). Let it stand 10 days, and draw it off carefully. Fine it down, and again rack it into another cask.

245. LONDON SHERRY WINE

12 pounds chopped raisins, 3 gallons soft water, 1 pound sugar, ½ ounce white tartar, 2 quarts cider. Let them stand together in a closed vessel one month; stir frequently. Then add 1 quart of spirits, ¼ pound wild cherries bruised. Let them stand 1 month longer and fine with isinglass.

246. STRAWBERRY WINE

12 gallons bruised strawberries, 10 gallons cider, 7 gallons water, 25 pounds sugar. Ferment, then add ½ ounce bruised orris root, ½ ounce bruised bitter almonds, ½ ounce bruised cloves, 6 ounces red tartar.

❖❖❖

247. CHAMPAGNE

The process of making American and imitation French champagne is one requiring great care, especially in producing a not only clear, but bright wine. Full directions are given below for making the necessary syrup, mixing the ingredients, fining, filtering and gassing; including a number of receipts for different kinds of champagne. A careful attention to the instructions laid down will produce wines which will compare favorably with the best genuine importations.

❖❖❖

248. TO MAKE A FILTER FOR FILTERING WINES

A filter for wines is usually made of felt, shaped like a cone or sugar loaf; those without any seam are the best. A lining of paper pulp is prepared in the following manner: Tear from 2 to 4 sheets filtering paper into small pieces and put it into a pail; pour over it a little boiling water, sufficient, by thorough beating, to form a fine smooth paste; then add sufficient water to fill the filter.

Pour this quickly into the filter, and, 5 minutes after the water has drained through, fill up with the wine to be filtered, taking care to keep the filter always full.

⬥⬥⬥

249. TO MAKE SYRUP FOR CHAMPAGNE WINE

To 25 pounds white sugar, add 2 gallons water and the whites of 4 eggs; stir until the sugar is dissolved. Let the whole simmer to the candy degree; then strain it through a bag made of fine flannel.

⬥⬥⬥

250. TO PREPARE ISINGLASS FOR FINING WINES

Cut up some isinglass (it must be of the very best quality), and put it in a jar, with just enough wine or water to cover it; add daily as much of the wine or water as has been absorbed by the isinglass. In 6 or 8 days it should be completely dissolved, forming a thick fluid mass. Squeeze it through a linen cloth and put it into a bottle, adding 4 or 5 per cent of 95 per cent alcohol to make it keep. For 40 gallons wine to be fined, take 1 wine-glassful of dissolved isinglass, add a little wine and a pinch of salt, and beat to a froth with a whisk, adding by degrees sufficient wine to make the mixture up to ½ gallon. When foaming, pour it slowly into the wine, stirring till all the fining is incorporated with the wine. Isinglass thus prepared and used will precipitate completely; and, after a few days, the wine will be bright. Too much care cannot be taken in the preparation of fining, as even the finest isinglass contains fibrous matter which dissolves with difficulty; this is very apt to remain suspended in the wine, and is not visible until developed, after bottling, by the gas with which the wine is afterwards charged.

❖❖❖

251. TO PREPARE CHAMPAGNE WINE FOR CHARGING

Put the wine used to make the champagne into a cask, add the brandy spirit, the aroma or flavoring, and the syrup, and stir for 10 minutes. Every day for 4 days draw off 15 or 20 gallons of the mixture and pour it in again; let it rest 4 days more, then add the fining, stir for 10 minutes, and bung up the cask. In 3 or 4 days if bright, draw off slowly, so as not to disturb the lees. Filter and it is ready for the fountain of the gassing apparatus.

❖❖❖

252. TO CHARGE CHAMPAGNE WITH GAS

Matthews' apparatus is the one usually adopted in the United States for generating the gas and charging champagne wine. The fountains, tubes, and valves are silver-lined, and the machines are adapted for pint and quart bottles. The following is a proper charge for a No. 2 apparatus with 2 fountains: Charge the generator with 9 gallons water, 6 gallons ground marble, and 3 gallons sulphuric acid; put 2 gallons water in the gas washer, and 20 gallons wine in each of the fountains. For a warm climate, a pressure of 70 pounds to the square inch is sufficient. When the wine is made in winter for immediate sale, the pressure may be increased to 80 pounds. Genuine champagne has an average pressure of 50 pounds.

◇–◇–◇

253. CALIFORNIA CHAMPAGNE

40 gallons California wine; 1 quart raspberry syrup; 4 gallons syrup made of 25 pounds sugar and 2 gallons water; and 4 gallons water. Or: 20 gallons California wine; 20 gallons Sauterne or white Bordeaux wine; ½ gallon old cognac brandy; with 4 gallons syrup as before. Add to these 10 per cent of water.

◇–◇–◇

254. IMITATION FRENCH CHAMPAGNE

40 gallons white Bordeaux wine; 1 gallon muscat wine; ½ gallon old cognac brandy; and 4 gallons syrup made of 25 pounds sugar and 2 gallons water. In this receipt a little tincture of vanilla, or a small bottle of bouquet venatique, may be used instead of the muscat wine. They may be omitted altogether if aroma is not desired.

255. CHEAP CHAMPAGNE

13 gallons California wine; 13 gallons white Bordeaux wine; 13 gallons water; 1 gallon 95 per cent French spirit; 1 quart raspberry syrup; and 4 gallons syrup made of 25 pounds sugar and 2 gallons water. Or: 20 gallons Catawba wine; 20 gallons water; 2 gallons Angelica wine; 2 gallons 95 per cent French spirit; and 4 gallons syrup made as before.

<><><>

256. THE USE OF GLYCERINE IN WINE

Glycerine differs from sugar in not fermenting or taking any active part in the process of fermentation. It can, however, be made use of after fermentation to impart any required degree of sweetness to wine, without the risk of further fermentation, as is the case with sugar when used for this purpose; it is said that it can be added with perfect safety to even a young or new wine, as soon as it has become clear. It is absolutely necessary that the glycerine should be chemically pure; care is consequently to be taken in purchasing it, as there are few articles in the market which are liable to contain so many impurities. The proportion of glycerine should be from 1 to 3 gallons for 100 gallons of wine, according to the quality of the latter. If the wine is perfectly clear before adding the glycerine it will be ready for bottling at once. It is best to mix the glycerine first with an equal quantity of the wine, and then add the mixture to the remainder of the wine.

257. ELECTRICITY AS AN AGENT FOR IM-PROVING WINES

From experiments made on a large scale, it has been found that electricity in any form, either as a regular current or a succession of discharges, renders wine or whiskey mellow and mature. It is supposed that the bitartrate of potassa is decomposed setting free potash and tartaric acid; the former tending to neutralize the acids of the wine; and the tartaric acid, reacting upon the fatty matters present, favors the formation of the ethers which constitute the bouquet of the wine. It is probable, also, that a small quantity of the water is decomposed, setting free oxygen, which forms, with some of the constituents of the wine, new compounds peculiar to old wines.

◇◇◇

258. HOME-MADE WINES

The various processes in domestic wine-making resemble those employed for foreign wine, and depend upon the same principles. The fruit should be preferably gathered in fine weather, and not till it has arrived at a proper state of maturity, as evinced by its flavor when tasted; for if it be employed while unripe, the wine will be harsh, disagreeable and unwholesome, and a larger quantity of sugar and spirit will be required to render it palatable. The common practice of employing unripe gooseberries for the manufacture of wine arises from a total ignorance of the scientific principles of wine making. On the other hand, if fruit be employed too ripe, the wine is apt to be inferior, and deficient in the flavor of the fruit. The fruit being gathered, it next undergoes the operation of picking, for the purpose of removing the stalks and unripe or damaged portion. It is next put in a tub and well bruised. Raisins are commonly permitted to soak about 24 hours previously to bruising them, or they may be advantageously bruised or minced in the dry state. The bruised fruit is then put into a vat or vessel with a guard or strainer placed over the tap-hole, to keep back the husks and seeds of the fruit when the must or juice is drawn off. The water is now added, and the whole macerated for 30 or 40 hours, more or less; during which time it is frequently stirred up with a suitable wooden stirrer. The liquid portion is next drawn off, and the residuary pulp is placed in hair bags and undergoes the operation of pressing to expel the fluid it contains. The sugar, tartar, etc. (in very fine powder or in solution), are now added to the mixed liquor, and the whole is well stirred. The temperature being suitable (generally from 75° to 85° Fahr.) the vinous fermentation soon commences, when the liquor is frequently skimmed (if necessary) and well stirred up, and after 3 or 4 days of this treatment, it is run into casks, which should be quite filled, and left open at the bung-hole. In about a week the flavoring ingredients, in the state of coarse powder, are commonly added, and well stirred in, and in about another week, depending upon the state of fermentation and the attenuation of the must, the brandy or spirit is added, and the cask filled up, and bunged down close. In 4 or 5 weeks more the cask is again filled up, and, after some weeks—the longer the better—it is "pegged" or "spiled" to ascertain if it be fine

or transparent; if so, it undergoes the operation of racking; but if, on the contrary, it still continues muddy, it
must previously pass through the process of fining. Its
future treatment is similar to that of foreign wine. The
must of many of the strong-flavored fruits, as black currants for instance, is improved by being boiled before
being made into wine; but the flower and bouquet of the
more delicate fruits are diminished, if not destroyed, by
boiling.

❖❖❖

259. GENERAL RECEIPT FOR THE PREPARA-
TION OF HOME-MADE WINE FROM RIPE
SACCHARINE FRUITS

I:—Ripe fruit, 4 pounds; clear soft water, 1 gallon;
sugar, 3 pounds; cream of tartar, dissolved in boiling
water, 1¼ ounces; brandy, 2 to 3 per cent. Flavoring as
required. Makes a good family wine.

II:—As the last, using 1 pound more each of fruit and
sugar. A superior wine.

III:—As the first, adding 2 pounds each fruit and
sugar. Very strong. Is good without brandy, but better
with it. 1½ pounds of raisins may be substituted for
each pound of sugar above. In the above way may be
made the following wines:—gooseberry wine, currant
wine (red, white or black); mixed fruit wine (currants
and gooseberries; or black, red, and white currants, ripe
black-heart cherries, and raspberries, equal parts). This is
a good family wine. Cherry wine; Colepress's wine (from
apples and mulberries, equal parts); elder wine; straw-

berry wine; raspberry wine; mulberry wine (when flavored makes port); whortleberry (sometimes called huckleberry) wine; makes a good factitious port; blackberry wine; morella wine; apricot wine; apple wine; grape wine, etc.

<><><>

260. GENERAL RECEIPT FOR MAKING WINE FROM DRY SACCHARINE FRUIT

I:—Dry fruit, 4½ pounds; soft water, 1 gallon; cream of tartar (dissolved), 1 pound; brandy, 1½ to 2 per cent, weak.

II:—As the last, but using 5½ pounds dried fruit. A superior family wine.

III:—As the last, 7½ pounds fruit, and brandy 3 per cent. A strong wine. Should the dried fruit employed be at all deficient in saccharine matter, 1 to 3 pounds may be omitted, and half that quantity of sugar, or two-thirds of raisins, added. In the above manner may be made raisin wine, fig wine, etc.

<><><>

261. IMITATION CHAMPAGNE

Stoned raisins, 7 pounds; loaf sugar, 21 pounds; water, 9 gallons; crystallized tartaric acid, 1 ounce; honey, ½ pound; ferment with sweet yeast 1 pound or less; skim frequently, and when the fermentation is nearly over, add coarse powdered orris root, 1 drachm, and eau de fleurs d'orange, 3 ounces; lemon juice, ¼ pint. Rack it, bung close, and in 3 months fine it down with isinglass, ½ ounce; in 1 month, if not sparkling, again fine it down, and in 2 weeks bottle it, observing to put a piece of double refined sugar, the size of a pea, into each bottle. The bottles should be wired, and the corks covered with tin foil.

◇◇◇

262. TO MAKE BLACKBERRY WINE

To make 10 gallons of this cheap and excellent wine, press the juice out of sufficient fresh ripe blackberries to make 4⅓ gallons; wash the pomace in 4⅓ gallons soft spring water, and thoroughly dissolve in it 6 pounds white sugar to each gallon of water (brown sugar will do for an inferior wine); strain the juice into this syrup, and mix them. Fill a cask with it perfectly full, and lay a cloth loosely over the bung-hole, placing the cask where it will be perfectly undisturbed. In 2 or 3 days fermentation will commence, and the impurities run over at the bung. Look at it every day, and if it does not run over, with some of the mixture which you have reserved in another vessel fill it up to the bung. In about 3 weeks, fermentation will have ceased, and the wine be still; fill it again, drive in the bung tight, nail a tin over it, and let it remain undisturbed until the following March. Then draw it off, without shaking the cask, put it into bottles, cork tightly and seal over. Some persons add spirit to the wine, but instead of doing good, it is only an injury. The more carefully the juice is strained, the better the quality of the sugar, and the more scrupulously clean the utensils and casks, the purer and better will be the wine.

—⋅⋅—

263. SPECIMEN PROCESS TO MAKE UNRIPE GRAPE, CURRANT, GOOSEBERRY AND RHUBARB WINE

according to the process of Dr. McCulloch. Gather the fruit when it is nearly full grown, but before it shows the least sign of ripening. Any kind will do, but it is advisable to avoid choosing those which, when ripe, would be highly flavored. All unsound and bruised fruit should be rejected, and the stalks and remains of blossom removed by picking or rubbing. The following receipt is one of the best on the subject: 40 pounds fruit are to be bruised in small quantities, in a tub which will hold 15 or 20 gallons, sufficient pressure only being used to burst the berries, without breaking the seeds or much compressing the skins. 4 gallons of water are then to be poured on the fruit, which is to be carefully stirred, and squeezed with the hands until the whole of the juice and pulp are separated from the solid matter. It is then to rest for a few hours, when it must be pressed and strained through a coarse canvas bag with considerable force. 1 gallon of water may afterwards be passed through the residue, to remove any soluble matter that may be left, and then added to the juice. 30 pounds loaf sugar are now to be dissolved in the juice, and the total quantity of liquid made up with water to 10½ gallons. The liquor is now to be put into a tub, over which spread a blanket, covered by a board, and place in a temperature of from 55° to 60° Fahr., for from 24 to 48 hours, according to the signs which it may show of fermentation, when it is to be put into a cask to ferment. The cask must be of such size that the liquor will nearly reach to the bung-hole, so that the scum may run out as it rises. As the fermentation goes on the liquor will decrease, and the cask must be kept filled up nearly to the bung-hole with a portion of the "must" which has been reserved for that purpose. When the fermentation has become a little weaker, which may be known by the hissing noise decreasing, the bung is to be driven in, and a wooden peg, called a spile, made of tough wood, put into a hole bored in the top of the barrel. After a few days this peg is to be loosened to let out any carbonic acid gas which has been generated. This must be done from time to time, and when there is no further sign of gas generating to the danger of the barrel, the spile may be made tight. The wine should be kept during the winter in a cool cellar, and, if fine, may be bottled on a clear cold day at the end of February or the beginning of March, without further trouble. But to ensure its fineness it is preferable to draw it off at the end of December into a fresh cask, so as to clear it from the lees. At this time, also, if it is found to be too sweet for the maker's taste, he should stir up the lees so as to renew the fermentation, at the same time raising the temperature. When it is transferred to the fresh cask, it should be fined with isinglass. Sometimes it is desirable to rack it off a second time into a fresh cask, again fining it. All these removals should be made in clear, dry, and if possible, cold weather. It must be bottled in March. This wine will usually be brisk, but circumstances will occasionally cause it to be sweet and still, and sometimes dry. If sweet, it may be re-made the following season, by adding to it juice from fresh fruit, according to the degree of sweetness, and fermenting and treating it as before. But if it be dry, briskness can never be restored, and it must be treated as a dry wine, by drawing it off into a cask previously fumigated with sulphur and fining and bottling it in the usual manner. Such dry wines sometimes taste disagreeably in the first and second year, but improve much with age. If the whole marc or husks, etc., is allowed to remain in the juice during the first fermentation, the process will be more rapid, and the wine stronger and less sweet; but it will have more flavor. If the wine is desired to be very sweet as well as brisk, 40 pounds of sugar may be used; less sweet and less strong, 25 pounds; it will be brisk, but not so strong, and ought to be used within a year.

❖❖❖

264. TO FINE WINE DIFFICULT TO CLARIFY, OR THICK IN CONSEQUENCE OF AN IMPERFECT FERMENTATION

To clarify 60 gallons, take 1 ounce of the species of Dock or Rumex plant, called Patience root, which boil in 1 quart water. When cold, filter, and add 1 ounce common salt, then 1 glass sheep's blood. Beat all the ingredients well together with a broom until the mixture foams up well, then add it gradually to the wine, stirring continually while pouring it in, and for 15 minutes afterwards. In a few days the wine will be clear.

265. TO FINE MADEIRA OR ANY KIND OF WINE WITH ISINGLASS

To fine 40 gallons wine, steep 1 ounce isinglass in 1 pint of pure cold water over night, and then melt it over a gentle charcoal fire, until a uniform gelatinous mass is formed. When cool, mix with it 3 pints wine, and let it repose 12 hours in a moderately warm room. Then add 1 gallon wine and mix the whole in a wooden vessel; whisk it with a clean broom until it foams up. Pour this mixture gradually in the wine you desire to fine, being careful to stir the whole continually during the process. Bung up the cask, and in the course of 48 hours the wine will appear perfectly clear and bright. Isinglass prepared in this way will precipitate perfectly, and leave no particles suspended in the wine.

⋄—⋄—⋄

266. TO FINE WHITE WINE WITH EGGS

To fine 60 gallons white wine, take the whites of 5 or 6 eggs, 1 egg-shell nearly reduced to powder, and a small handful of common salt. Beat the whole together in a little of the wine, with a small clean broom, until it foams, then pour it into the wine gradually, constantly stirring it all the while.

⋄—⋄—⋄

267. TO FINE RED WINE

This is clarified in the same way. When you have Roussillon, or the dark wines called vin du midi, which are usually of a deep color, and wish to make it of a lighter

color, add 5 or 6 eggs, yellows, whites, and shells together, with a small handful of salt.

◇◇◇

268. TO FINE A PIPE OF PORT WINE

Take the whites and shells of ten good eggs, and beat
them up to a froth in a wooden bucket; add 1 gallon of
Port and whisk it well up to a froth with a clean broom;
draw off 4 gallons, and put the finings in it; stir it up well;
leaving out the bung one day; then bung it up, and in 10
days it will be fit to bottle. If the weather be warm, mix up
1 pint silver sand and to the finings.

◇◇◇

269. TO REMEDY ROPINESS IN WINE

The peculiar cloudy, stringy, oily appearance in wine,
called by the French "graisse," and by the American "ropiness" is occasioned by the presence of a glutinous substance, and is generally observed in those white wines
which do not contain much tannin. M. François, a chemist
first discovered the cause, and pointed out the proper
remedy, in the addition of tannin. He recommended the
use of 1 pound of the bruised berries of the mountain ash
in a somewhat unripe state, well stirred in each barrel of
the wine to be improved. After agitation, the wine is to be
left to repose a day or two, and then racked off. The tannin in the berries by this time will have separated and
precipitated the glutinous matter from the liquid, and re-

moved the ropiness. Wines thus affected cannot be fined
in the regular way, as they do not contain sufficient of the
astringent principle to cause the coagulation or precipitation of the finings; this principle must therefore be sup-
plied, and for pale white wines, which are the kind chiefly
attacked with ropiness, nothing equals a little pure tannin
or tannic acid dissolved in proof spirit. Red wines contain
so much tannic acid that they are never troubled by ropiness. Wine, after having been cured of ropiness, should
immediately be fined and bottled.

270. TO RIPEN WINE

Dealers adopt various ways to hasten the ripening of
wine. One of the safest and best plans for this purpose,
especially for strong wines, is to let them remain on the
lees 15 to 18 months before racking off, or, whether
"crude" or "racked," keeping them at a temperature rang-
ing between 50° to 60° Fahr. in a cellar free from
draught, and not too dry. Dealers sometimes remove the
bungs or corks, and substitute bladders fastened air-tight.
Bottled wine treated in this way, and kept at about 70°
Fahr. ripens very rapidly. 4 or 5 drops of acetic acid added
to a bottle of some kinds of new wine, immediately gives
it the appearance of being 2 or 3 years old.

271. TO REMEDY SOUR WINE

The souring of wine is produced by various circumstances, sometimes from its having been kept in a warm

cellar where it has been exposed to draughts of air, often by the vibration occasioned by the rolling of heavy bodies over the cellar; but most frequently it originates from the wine having been imperfectly fermented. The only safe remedy for the souring of wine is the cautious addition of a little neutral tartrate of potash; it may also be mixed with a larger quantity of rich wine of its kind, at the same time adding a little good brandy. Wine treated in this way should be fined after having stood 2 or 3 weeks, and then immediately bottled, and consumed as soon as possible, for it will never prove a good keeping wine.

⟡⟡⟡

272. TO RESTORE PRICKED OR DECAYING WINE

If the wine is only thick, add 2 pints of milk to every 30 gallons of wine, and stir 10 minutes. But if the wine has an inferior taste, or is partly or entirely spoiled, treat it as follows: Put the 30 gallons wine into a clean cask, then take 2 pints spirit of wine, 95 per cent; 3 ounces common salt; 1 pound white sugar. Dissolve the salt and sugar in ½ gallon of the wine, and add the spirit. Then pour the whole gradually into the wine, being careful to stir it continually with a stick during the operation. After the mixture is all poured into the wine, stir the whole for 10 minutes longer. Then add 2 pints milk and continue stirring 10 minutes more. After some days the wine will be completely clarified and restored. "Pricked" wine signifies wine which has been slightly soured.

273. TO REMEDY EXCESSIVE ACIDITY IN GERMAN WINE

Simply add a little chalk. This mode of correcting the sourness of wine is perfectly harmless, whereas the pernicious practice of using white and vitrified lead for this purpose cannot be too much condemned. Lead in any form is a poison.

◇–◇–◇

274. TO RESTORE SOUR WINE WITH POTASH

To 25 gallons wine, add 4 ounces potash dissolved in a little water, and stir well with a stick for 10 minutes.

◇–◇–◇

275. TO TEST WINES BEGINNING TO DECOMPOSE

Many persons are unaware of the difference between a wine that is beginning to decompose (called in French the Poux), and that in which the acetous fermentation has commenced. The Poux appears at the bottom of the barrel, while acetification begins at the top. For the first stage of the Poux the wine becomes thick, and has a peculiar taste termed flat. For the second stage the wine becomes still more troubled, and has the taste of stagnant water. Finally, in the last stage, when the decomposition has reached its maximum, the wine becomes grayish and appears like muddy water. If some of the wine is put into a champagne glass and a pinch of tartaric acid is added, a red color will be produced, which will not be the case if the wine is in a state of acetous fermentation.

276. TO REMOVE MUSTINESS FROM WINE

The disagreeable taste in wine, generally known as mustiness, is occasioned by the presence of an essential oil. This may be removed by adding a little sweet or almond oil, and then violently stirring the wine for some time. The fixed oil attracts and seizes on the essential oil, and rises with it to the surface, when it is easily skimmed off, or the liquid under it drawn off. A few slices of burnt or toasted bread, or a little bruised mustard seed or coarsely powdered charcoal, will often have the same effect.

⋄⋄⋄

277. PASTEUR'S METHOD OF PRESERVING WINES

M. Pasteur announced some time ago that wines became spoiled in consequence of the presence of microscopic organisms, which could be destroyed by exposing the wine, for a few moments only, to a temperature of 131° Fahr. A committee of experts was appointed to make a comparative examination of wines which had and which had not been subjected to heat; M. Lapparent being President, and M. Dumas and M. Pasteur assisting. They concluded that the preservation of wine in bottles is greatly improved by heating; that the destruction of the germs is perfect, without the least impairment of the taste, color or limpidity of the wines.

278. TO DETERMINE THE NATURE OF ACIDITY IN WINE

If wine has undergone the acetous fermentation, then convert it at once into vinegar by one of the usual modes. But if its acidity proceeds from an excess of tartaric acid, this defect may be remedied by shaking the wine with a concentrated solution of neutral tartrate of potassa, which, with the surplus of tartaric acid, will form bitartrate of potassa, and precipitate as such. To discover the nature of the acidity, neutralize an ounce or so of the wine with some carbonate of soda, then add a small quantity of sulphuric acid, and boil up; if acetic acid or vinegar be present, it will be perceptible by its odor.

❖❖❖

279. PARENT'S METHOD OF PRESERVING WINE

This consists in the addition of a small quantity of tannin or tannic acid to the wine, which perhaps acts in a similar way, by destroying the vitality of the spores of the fungus, since a microscopic examination of wine known to contain these germs, within a few weeks after being treated with the tannin, has failed to detect the slightest trace. Indeed, wine which has already begun to change, and become turbid, can be restored to its primitive clearness, and with a great improvement in its taste. Care must be taken, however, to use only tannin which has been prepared from the constituents of the grape, since the slightest proportion of the extract of nut-gall, although accomplishing the general object of destroying the fungus, will impart a peculiar taste, which never disappears.

◇◇◇

280. ANTIFERMENTS FOR CIDER, WINE, MALT LIQUORS, ETC.

Grind or bruise together 13 pounds new mustard seed and 1 pound cloves. This mixture may be used with or without the addition of 10 ounces ground capsicum.

◇◇◇

281. TO INDUCE FERMENTATION

If fermentation does not begin within a reasonable time, raise the temperature by covering the vessel with blankets, and moving it near to a fire. Or, warm a portion of the must and add it to the rest. A small quantity of yeast, previously well mixed with some of the liquor, gently stirred in, will have the same effect. Or, the must may be warmed by placing large stone bottles, fitted with boiling water and well corked, in the liquor.

◇◇◇

282. TO ARREST FERMENTATION

Dip a strip of linen or cotton, an inch wide and seven inches long, into melted sulphur. Fasten a wire into the bung of a 60 gallon cask, so that the end will hang about the middle of the inside of the cask, bend the end up to form a hook, place the sulphur tape on the hook, ignite it, and insert it in the cask, bunging loosely. In about an hour the cask will be impregnated with sulphurous acid; then withdraw the match, and fill up with wine, and bung up tight. This will stop further fermentation. This is a good plan for white wines, but not for red wines, as sulphur injures their color. Sulphite (not sulphate) of lime is also sometimes employed to arrest fermentation.

<><><>

283. HAHNEMANN'S TEST FOR LEAD IN WINE

Take 1 ounce quicklime, 1½ ounces flowers of sulphur; heat in a covered crucible for 5 or 6 minutes; take 2 drachms of this compound (which is sulphuret of lime), 2 drachms of tartaric acid; powder, mix, and shake in a stoppered bottle with a pint of water; let it settle, pour off the clear liquid, and add 1½ ounces tartaric acid. The above test will throw down the least quantity of lead from wines, as a very sensible black precipitate.

<><><>

284. PARIS TEST FOR LEAD IN WINE

Expose equal parts of sulphur and powdered oyster shells to a white heat for 15 minutes, and, when cold, add an equal quantity of cream of tartar; these are to be put into a strong bottle, with common water, to boil for an hour, and the solution is afterwards to be decanted into ounce phials, adding 20 drops muriatic acid to each. Both the above tests will throw down the least quantity of lead from wines, as a very sensible black precipitate. As iron might be accidentally contained in the wine, the muriatic acid is added to prevent the precipitation of that metal. This acts in the same manner as Hahnemann's test.

◇—◇—◇

285. TO DISTINGUISH ARTIFICIALLY COLORED WINES

As the real coloring matter of wine is of difficult solubility in water free from tartaric acid, Blume proposes to make this fact of practical use in testing the purity of wine. A crumb of bread saturated in the supposed wine is placed in a plate of water; if artificially colored, the water soon partakes of the color; but if natural, a slight opalescence only will be perceptible after a quarter of an hour.

◇—◇—◇

286. TO DETECT LOGWOOD IN WINE

M. Lapeymere, having observed that haematine, the coloring principle of logwood, gives a sky-blue color in the presence of salts of copper, proposes the following test for logwood in wines: Paper is saturated with a strong solution of neutral acetate of copper, and dried. A strip of this is dipped into the suspected liquor, and, after removal, the adhering drops are made to move to and fro over the paper, which is finally to be carefully dried. If the wine contain logwood, the paper will assume a violet-blue color; but if the wine possess its natural coloring matter the paper will have a grey tint.

◇◆◇

287. TO DETECT ARTIFICIAL COLORING IN WINE

Use, as test liquid, a solution of potash and a solution of liquid ammonia and potash. If the wine is colored by the coloring matter of the grape, potash changes the red color to a bottle green or brownish-green; ammonia changes the color to brownish-green or greenish-brown; a solution of alum to which some potash has been added gives a dirty grey precipitate.

If the wine is artificially colored, potash gives the following colored precipitates: Dark elder, mulberry, or beet root gives a violet precipitate; pokewood berries, a yellow; Indian wood, a violet red; pernambuco, a red; litmus, a violet blue; orchil or cudbear, a dirty lees color.

Or: Pour into the wine to be tested a solution of alum, and precipitate the alumina it contains, by adding potash, and the precipitates will have the same characteristics as above.

◇◆◇

288. GRAPE CHAMPAGNE

Gather the grapes when they are just turning or about half ripe; pound them in a tub, and to every quart of pounded fruit add 2 quarts of water. Let it stand in the mash-tub for 14 days, then draw it off, and to every gallon of liquor add 3 pounds of loaf sugar. When the sugar is dissolved, cask it; and, after it has done working, bring it down. In 6 months it should be bottled, and the corks tied down or wired. This produces a domestic real champagne in no way inferior to the genuine imported article.

◇—◇—◇

289. IMITATION WHITE FRONTIGNAC WINE

Boil 18 pounds white powdered sugar, with 6 gallons water, and the whites of 2 eggs well beaten; then skim it, and put in ¼ peck elder flower from the tree that bears white berries; do not keep them on the fire. When nearly cold, stir it, and put in 6 spoonfuls lemon juice, 4 or 5 of yeast, and beat well into the liquor; stir it every day; put 6 pounds best raisins, stoned, into the cask, and tun the wine. Stop it close, and bottle in 6 months. When well kept this wine is an excellent imitation of Frontignac.

◇—◇—◇

290. IMITATION RED FRONTIGNAC WINE

This is made in the same manner, and with the same ingredients as the white wine, except that dark elder flowers are used instead of white.

INDEX

HOME MADE BRANDIES

HOME MADE CORDIALS

HOME MADE GIN

HOME MADE MIXED DRINKS

ELEVEN FAMOUS COCKTAILS

HOME MADE WINES

Printed in Great Britain
by Amazon

33863594R00088